C-2499　　CAREER EXAMINATION SERIES

This is your
PASSBOOK for...

Senior Maintenance Mechanic

Test Preparation Study Guide
Questions & Answers

COPYRIGHT NOTICE

This book is SOLELY intended for, is sold ONLY to, and its use is RESTRICTED to individual, bona fide applicants or candidates who qualify by virtue of having seriously filed applications for appropriate license, certificate, professional and/or promotional advancement, higher school matriculation, scholarship, or other legitimate requirements of education and/or governmental authorities.

This book is NOT intended for use, class instruction, tutoring, training, duplication, copying, reprinting, excerption, or adaptation, etc., by:

1) Other publishers
2) Proprietors and/or Instructors of "Coaching" and/or Preparatory Courses
3) Personnel and/or Training Divisions of commercial, industrial, and governmental organizations
4) Schools, colleges, or universities and/or their departments and staffs, including teachers and other personnel
5) Testing Agencies or Bureaus
6) Study groups which seek by the purchase of a single volume to copy and/or duplicate and/or adapt this material for use by the group as a whole without having purchased individual volumes for each of the members of the group
7) Et al.

Such persons would be in violation of appropriate Federal and State statutes.

PROVISION OF LICENSING AGREEMENTS – Recognized educational, commercial, industrial, and governmental institutions and organizations, and others legitimately engaged in educational pursuits, including training, testing, and measurement activities, may address request for a licensing agreement to the copyright owners, who will determine whether, and under what conditions, including fees and charges, the materials in this book may be used them. In other words, a licensing facility exists for the legitimate use of the material in this book on other than an individual basis. However, it is asseverated and affirmed here that the material in this book CANNOT be used without the receipt of the express permission of such a licensing agreement from the Publishers. Inquiries re licensing should be addressed to the company, attention rights and permissions department.

All rights reserved, including the right of reproduction in whole or in part, in any form or by any means, electronic or mechanical, including photocopying, recording, or by any information storage and retrieval system, without permission in writing from the Publisher.

Copyright © 2025 by
National Learning Corporation

212 Michael Drive, Syosset, NY 11791
(516) 921-8888 • www.passbooks.com
E-mail: info@passbooks.com

PASSBOOK® SERIES

THE *PASSBOOK® SERIES* has been created to prepare applicants and candidates for the ultimate academic battlefield – the examination room.

At some time in our lives, each and every one of us may be required to take an examination – for validation, matriculation, admission, qualification, registration, certification, or licensure.

Based on the assumption that every applicant or candidate has met the basic formal educational standards, has taken the required number of courses, and read the necessary texts, the *PASSBOOK® SERIES* furnishes the one special preparation which may assure passing with confidence, instead of failing with insecurity. Examination questions – together with answers – are furnished as the basic vehicle for study so that the mysteries of the examination and its compounding difficulties may be eliminated or diminished by a sure method.

This book is meant to help you pass your examination provided that you qualify and are serious in your objective.

The entire field is reviewed through the huge store of content information which is succinctly presented through a provocative and challenging approach – the question-and-answer method.

A climate of success is established by furnishing the correct answers at the end of each test.

You soon learn to recognize types of questions, forms of questions, and patterns of questioning. You may even begin to anticipate expected outcomes.

You perceive that many questions are repeated or adapted so that you can gain acute insights, which may enable you to score many sure points.

You learn how to confront new questions, or types of questions, and to attack them confidently and work out the correct answers.

You note objectives and emphases, and recognize pitfalls and dangers, so that you may make positive educational adjustments.

Moreover, you are kept fully informed in relation to new concepts, methods, practices, and directions in the field.

You discover that you are actually taking the examination all the time: you are preparing for the examination by "taking" an examination, not by reading extraneous and/or supererogatory textbooks.

In short, this PASSBOOK®, used directedly, should be an important factor in helping you to pass your test.

SENIOR MAINTENANCE MECHANIC

DUTIES
Has responsible charge of the maintenance and operation of buildings, grounds and equipment; supervises all maintenance personnel; makes periodic inspection of properties; supervises or assists in the repair of plumbing and heating equipment; supervises or performs work in carpentry, painting, masonry, roofing, tiling, locksmithing and other mechanical work; maintains and cares for landscaped areas; estimates materials required for repairs; keeps time and material records; reads utility meters; requisitions supplies; performs a variety of other skilled work.

SUBJECT OF EXAMINATION
Written test will be designed to measure knowledge, skills, and/or abilities in such areas as:
1. Building maintenance and repair;
2. Building trades, including mechanical and electrical;
3. Tools and their uses;
4. Operation and maintenance of heating, air conditioning and ventilating systems; and
5. Supervision.

HOW TO TAKE A TEST

I. YOU MUST PASS AN EXAMINATION

A. WHAT EVERY CANDIDATE SHOULD KNOW

Examination applicants often ask us for help in preparing for the written test. What can I study in advance? What kinds of questions will be asked? How will the test be given? How will the papers be graded?

As an applicant for a civil service examination, you may be wondering about some of these things. Our purpose here is to suggest effective methods of advance study and to describe civil service examinations.

Your chances for success on this examination can be increased if you know how to prepare. Those "pre-examination jitters" can be reduced if you know what to expect. You can even experience an adventure in good citizenship if you know why civil service exams are given.

B. WHY ARE CIVIL SERVICE EXAMINATIONS GIVEN?

Civil service examinations are important to you in two ways. As a citizen, you want public jobs filled by employees who know how to do their work. As a job seeker, you want a fair chance to compete for that job on an equal footing with other candidates. The best-known means of accomplishing this two-fold goal is the competitive examination.

Exams are widely publicized throughout the nation. They may be administered for jobs in federal, state, city, municipal, town or village governments or agencies.

Any citizen may apply, with some limitations, such as the age or residence of applicants. Your experience and education may be reviewed to see whether you meet the requirements for the particular examination. When these requirements exist, they are reasonable and applied consistently to all applicants. Thus, a competitive examination may cause you some uneasiness now, but it is your privilege and safeguard.

C. HOW ARE CIVIL SERVICE EXAMS DEVELOPED?

Examinations are carefully written by trained technicians who are specialists in the field known as "psychological measurement," in consultation with recognized authorities in the field of work that the test will cover. These experts recommend the subject matter areas or skills to be tested; only those knowledges or skills important to your success on the job are included. The most reliable books and source materials available are used as references. Together, the experts and technicians judge the difficulty level of the questions.

Test technicians know how to phrase questions so that the problem is clearly stated. Their ethics do not permit "trick" or "catch" questions. Questions may have been tried out on sample groups, or subjected to statistical analysis, to determine their usefulness.

Written tests are often used in combination with performance tests, ratings of training and experience, and oral interviews. All of these measures combine to form the best-known means of finding the right person for the right job.

II. HOW TO PASS THE WRITTEN TEST

A. NATURE OF THE EXAMINATION

To prepare intelligently for civil service examinations, you should know how they differ from school examinations you have taken. In school you were assigned certain definite pages to read or subjects to cover. The examination questions were quite detailed and usually emphasized memory. Civil service exams, on the other hand, try to discover your present ability to perform the duties of a position, plus your potentiality to learn these duties. In other words, a civil service exam attempts to predict how successful you will be. Questions cover such a broad area that they cannot be as minute and detailed as school exam questions.

In the public service similar kinds of work, or positions, are grouped together in one "class." This process is known as *position-classification*. All the positions in a class are paid according to the salary range for that class. One class title covers all of these positions, and they are all tested by the same examination.

B. FOUR BASIC STEPS

1) Study the announcement

How, then, can you know what subjects to study? Our best answer is: "Learn as much as possible about the class of positions for which you've applied." The exam will test the knowledge, skills and abilities needed to do the work.

Your most valuable source of information about the position you want is the official exam announcement. This announcement lists the training and experience qualifications. Check these standards and apply only if you come reasonably close to meeting them.

The brief description of the position in the examination announcement offers some clues to the subjects which will be tested. Think about the job itself. Review the duties in your mind. Can you perform them, or are there some in which you are rusty? Fill in the blank spots in your preparation.

Many jurisdictions preview the written test in the exam announcement by including a section called "Knowledge and Abilities Required," "Scope of the Examination," or some similar heading. Here you will find out specifically what fields will be tested.

2) Review your own background

Once you learn in general what the position is all about, and what you need to know to do the work, ask yourself which subjects you already know fairly well and which need improvement. You may wonder whether to concentrate on improving your strong areas or on building some background in your fields of weakness. When the announcement has specified "some knowledge" or "considerable knowledge," or has used adjectives like "beginning principles of..." or "advanced ... methods," you can get a clue as to the number and difficulty of questions to be asked in any given field. More questions, and hence broader coverage, would be included for those subjects which are more important in the work. Now weigh your strengths and weaknesses against the job requirements and prepare accordingly.

3) Determine the level of the position

Another way to tell how intensively you should prepare is to understand the level of the job for which you are applying. Is it the entering level? In other words, is this the position in which beginners in a field of work are hired? Or is it an intermediate or advanced level? Sometimes this is indicated by such words as "Junior" or "Senior" in the class title. Other jurisdictions use Roman numerals to designate the level – Clerk I, Clerk II, for example. The word "Supervisor" sometimes appears in the title. If the level is not indicated by the title, check the description of duties. Will you be working under very close supervision, or will you have responsibility for independent decisions in this work?

4) Choose appropriate study materials

Now that you know the subjects to be examined and the relative amount of each subject to be covered, you can choose suitable study materials. For beginning level jobs, or even advanced ones, if you have a pronounced weakness in some aspect of your training, read a modern, standard textbook in that field. Be sure it is up to date and has general coverage. Such books are normally available at your library, and the librarian will be glad to help you locate one. For entry-level positions, questions of appropriate difficulty are chosen – neither highly advanced questions, nor those too simple. Such questions require careful thought but not advanced training.

If the position for which you are applying is technical or advanced, you will read more advanced, specialized material. If you are already familiar with the basic principles of your field, elementary textbooks would waste your time. Concentrate on advanced textbooks and technical periodicals. Think through the concepts and review difficult problems in your field.

These are all general sources. You can get more ideas on your own initiative, following these leads. For example, training manuals and publications of the government agency which employs workers in your field can be useful, particularly for technical and professional positions. A letter or visit to the government department involved may result in more specific study suggestions, and certainly will provide you with a more definite idea of the exact nature of the position you are seeking.

III. KINDS OF TESTS

Tests are used for purposes other than measuring knowledge and ability to perform specified duties. For some positions, it is equally important to test ability to make adjustments to new situations or to profit from training. In others, basic mental abilities not dependent on information are essential. Questions which test these things may not appear as pertinent to the duties of the position as those which test for knowledge and information. Yet they are often highly important parts of a fair examination. For very general questions, it is almost impossible to help you direct your study efforts. What we can do is to point out some of the more common of these general abilities needed in public service positions and describe some typical questions.

1) General information

Broad, general information has been found useful for predicting job success in some kinds of work. This is tested in a variety of ways, from vocabulary lists to questions about current events. Basic background in some field of work, such as sociology or economics, may be sampled in a group of questions. Often these are principles which have become familiar to most persons through exposure rather than through formal training. It is difficult to advise you how to study for these questions; being alert to the world around you is our best suggestion.

2) Verbal ability

An example of an ability needed in many positions is verbal or language ability. Verbal ability is, in brief, the ability to use and understand words. Vocabulary and grammar tests are typical measures of this ability. Reading comprehension or paragraph interpretation questions are common in many kinds of civil service tests. You are given a paragraph of written material and asked to find its central meaning.

3) Numerical ability

Number skills can be tested by the familiar arithmetic problem, by checking paired lists of numbers to see which are alike and which are different, or by interpreting charts and graphs. In the latter test, a graph may be printed in the test booklet which you are asked to use as the basis for answering questions.

4) Observation

A popular test for law-enforcement positions is the observation test. A picture is shown to you for several minutes, then taken away. Questions about the picture test your ability to observe both details and larger elements.

5) Following directions

In many positions in the public service, the employee must be able to carry out written instructions dependably and accurately. You may be given a chart with several columns, each column listing a variety of information. The questions require you to carry out directions involving the information given in the chart.

6) Skills and aptitudes

Performance tests effectively measure some manual skills and aptitudes. When the skill is one in which you are trained, such as typing or shorthand, you can practice. These tests are often very much like those given in business school or high school courses. For many of the other skills and aptitudes, however, no short-time preparation can be made. Skills and abilities natural to you or that you have developed throughout your lifetime are being tested.

Many of the general questions just described provide all the data needed to answer the questions and ask you to use your reasoning ability to find the answers. Your best preparation for these tests, as well as for tests of facts and ideas, is to be at your physical and mental best. You, no doubt, have your own methods of getting into an exam-taking mood and keeping "in shape." The next section lists some ideas on this subject.

IV. KINDS OF QUESTIONS

Only rarely is the "essay" question, which you answer in narrative form, used in civil service tests. Civil service tests are usually of the short-answer type. Full instructions for answering these questions will be given to you at the examination. But in case this is your first experience with short-answer questions and separate answer sheets, here is what you need to know:

1) **Multiple-choice Questions**

Most popular of the short-answer questions is the "multiple choice" or "best answer" question. It can be used, for example, to test for factual knowledge, ability to solve problems or judgment in meeting situations found at work.

A multiple-choice question is normally one of three types—
- It can begin with an incomplete statement followed by several possible endings. You are to find the one ending which *best* completes the statement, although some of the others may not be entirely wrong.
- It can also be a complete statement in the form of a question which is answered by choosing one of the statements listed.

- It can be in the form of a problem – again you select the best answer.

Here is an example of a multiple-choice question with a discussion which should give you some clues as to the method for choosing the right answer:

When an employee has a complaint about his assignment, the action which will *best* help him overcome his difficulty is to
    A. discuss his difficulty with his coworkers
    B. take the problem to the head of the organization
    C. take the problem to the person who gave him the assignment
    D. say nothing to anyone about his complaint

In answering this question, you should study each of the choices to find which is best. Consider choice "A" – Certainly an employee may discuss his complaint with fellow employees, but no change or improvement can result, and the complaint remains unresolved. Choice "B" is a poor choice since the head of the organization probably does not know what assignment you have been given, and taking your problem to him is known as "going over the head" of the supervisor. The supervisor, or person who made the assignment, is the person who can clarify it or correct any injustice. Choice "C" is, therefore, correct. To say nothing, as in choice "D," is unwise. Supervisors have and interest in knowing the problems employees are facing, and the employee is seeking a solution to his problem.

2) True/False Questions

The "true/false" or "right/wrong" form of question is sometimes used. Here a complete statement is given. Your job is to decide whether the statement is right or wrong.

SAMPLE: A roaming cell-phone call to a nearby city costs less than a non-roaming call to a distant city.

This statement is wrong, or false, since roaming calls are more expensive.

This is not a complete list of all possible question forms, although most of the others are variations of these common types. You will always get complete directions for answering questions. Be sure you understand *how* to mark your answers – ask questions until you do.

V. RECORDING YOUR ANSWERS

Computer terminals are used more and more today for many different kinds of exams.
For an examination with very few applicants, you may be told to record your answers in the test booklet itself. Separate answer sheets are much more common. If this separate answer sheet is to be scored by machine – and this is often the case – it is highly important that you mark your answers correctly in order to get credit.
An electronic scoring machine is often used in civil service offices because of the speed with which papers can be scored. Machine-scored answer sheets must be marked with a pencil, which will be given to you. This pencil has a high graphite content which responds to the electronic scoring machine. As a matter of fact, stray dots may register as answers, so do not let your pencil rest on the answer sheet while you are pondering the correct answer. Also, if your pencil lead breaks or is otherwise defective, ask for another.

Since the answer sheet will be dropped in a slot in the scoring machine, be careful not to bend the corners or get the paper crumpled.

The answer sheet normally has five vertical columns of numbers, with 30 numbers to a column. These numbers correspond to the question numbers in your test booklet. After each number, going across the page are four or five pairs of dotted lines. These short dotted lines have small letters or numbers above them. The first two pairs may also have a "T" or "F" above the letters. This indicates that the first two pairs only are to be used if the questions are of the true-false type. If the questions are multiple choice, disregard the "T" and "F" and pay attention only to the small letters or numbers.

Answer your questions in the manner of the sample that follows:

32. The largest city in the United States is
    A. Washington, D.C.
    B. New York City
    C. Chicago
    D. Detroit
    E. San Francisco

1) Choose the answer you think is best. (New York City is the largest, so "B" is correct.)
2) Find the row of dotted lines numbered the same as the question you are answering. (Find row number 32)
3) Find the pair of dotted lines corresponding to the answer. (Find the pair of lines under the mark "B.")
4) Make a solid black mark between the dotted lines.

VI. BEFORE THE TEST

Common sense will help you find procedures to follow to get ready for an examination. Too many of us, however, overlook these sensible measures. Indeed, nervousness and fatigue have been found to be the most serious reasons why applicants fail to do their best on civil service tests. Here is a list of reminders:

- Begin your preparation early – Don't wait until the last minute to go scurrying around for books and materials or to find out what the position is all about.
- Prepare continuously – An hour a night for a week is better than an all-night cram session. This has been definitely established. What is more, a night a week for a month will return better dividends than crowding your study into a shorter period of time.
- Locate the place of the exam – You have been sent a notice telling you when and where to report for the examination. If the location is in a different town or otherwise unfamiliar to you, it would be well to inquire the best route and learn something about the building.
- Relax the night before the test – Allow your mind to rest. Do not study at all that night. Plan some mild recreation or diversion; then go to bed early and get a good night's sleep.
- Get up early enough to make a leisurely trip to the place for the test – This way unforeseen events, traffic snarls, unfamiliar buildings, etc. will not upset you.
- Dress comfortably – A written test is not a fashion show. You will be known by number and not by name, so wear something comfortable.

- Leave excess paraphernalia at home – Shopping bags and odd bundles will get in your way. You need bring only the items mentioned in the official notice you received; usually everything you need is provided. Do not bring reference books to the exam. They will only confuse those last minutes and be taken away from you when in the test room.
- Arrive somewhat ahead of time – If because of transportation schedules you must get there very early, bring a newspaper or magazine to take your mind off yourself while waiting.
- Locate the examination room – When you have found the proper room, you will be directed to the seat or part of the room where you will sit. Sometimes you are given a sheet of instructions to read while you are waiting. Do not fill out any forms until you are told to do so; just read them and be prepared.
- Relax and prepare to listen to the instructions
- If you have any physical problem that may keep you from doing your best, be sure to tell the test administrator. If you are sick or in poor health, you really cannot do your best on the exam. You can come back and take the test some other time.

VII. AT THE TEST

The day of the test is here and you have the test booklet in your hand. The temptation to get going is very strong. Caution! There is more to success than knowing the right answers. You must know how to identify your papers and understand variations in the type of short-answer question used in this particular examination. Follow these suggestions for maximum results from your efforts:

1) Cooperate with the monitor

The test administrator has a duty to create a situation in which you can be as much at ease as possible. He will give instructions, tell you when to begin, check to see that you are marking your answer sheet correctly, and so on. He is not there to guard you, although he will see that your competitors do not take unfair advantage. He wants to help you do your best.

2) Listen to all instructions

Don't jump the gun! Wait until you understand all directions. In most civil service tests you get more time than you need to answer the questions. So don't be in a hurry. Read each word of instructions until you clearly understand the meaning. Study the examples, listen to all announcements and follow directions. Ask questions if you do not understand what to do.

3) Identify your papers

Civil service exams are usually identified by number only. You will be assigned a number; you must not put your name on your test papers. Be sure to copy your number correctly. Since more than one exam may be given, copy your exact examination title.

4) Plan your time

Unless you are told that a test is a "speed" or "rate of work" test, speed itself is usually not important. Time enough to answer all the questions will be provided, but this does not mean that you have all day. An overall time limit has been set. Divide the total time (in minutes) by the number of questions to determine the approximate time you have for each question.

5) Do not linger over difficult questions

If you come across a difficult question, mark it with a paper clip (useful to have along) and come back to it when you have been through the booklet. One caution if you do this – be sure to skip a number on your answer sheet as well. Check often to be sure that you have not lost your place and that you are marking in the row numbered the same as the question you are answering.

6) Read the questions

Be sure you know what the question asks! Many capable people are unsuccessful because they failed to *read* the questions correctly.

7) Answer all questions

Unless you have been instructed that a penalty will be deducted for incorrect answers, it is better to guess than to omit a question.

8) Speed tests

It is often better NOT to guess on speed tests. It has been found that on timed tests people are tempted to spend the last few seconds before time is called in marking answers at random – without even reading them – in the hope of picking up a few extra points. To discourage this practice, the instructions may warn you that your score will be "corrected" for guessing. That is, a penalty will be applied. The incorrect answers will be deducted from the correct ones, or some other penalty formula will be used.

9) Review your answers

If you finish before time is called, go back to the questions you guessed or omitted to give them further thought. Review other answers if you have time.

10) Return your test materials

If you are ready to leave before others have finished or time is called, take ALL your materials to the monitor and leave quietly. Never take any test material with you. The monitor can discover whose papers are not complete, and taking a test booklet may be grounds for disqualification.

VIII. EXAMINATION TECHNIQUES

1) Read the general instructions carefully. These are usually printed on the first page of the exam booklet. As a rule, these instructions refer to the timing of the examination; the fact that you should not start work until the signal and must stop work at a signal, etc. If there are any *special* instructions, such as a choice of questions to be answered, make sure that you note this instruction carefully.

2) When you are ready to start work on the examination, that is as soon as the signal has been given, read the instructions to each question booklet, underline any key words or phrases, such as *least, best, outline, describe* and the like. In this way you will tend to answer as requested rather than discover on reviewing your paper that you *listed without describing*, that you selected the *worst* choice rather than the *best* choice, etc.

3) If the examination is of the objective or multiple-choice type – that is, each question will also give a series of possible answers: A, B, C or D, and you are called upon to select the best answer and write the letter next to that answer on your answer paper – it is advisable to start answering each question in turn. There may be anywhere from 50 to 100 such questions in the three or four hours allotted and you can see how much time would be taken if you read through all the questions before beginning to answer any. Furthermore, if you come across a question or group of questions which you know would be difficult to answer, it would undoubtedly affect your handling of all the other questions.

4) If the examination is of the essay type and contains but a few questions, it is a moot point as to whether you should read all the questions before starting to answer any one. Of course, if you are given a choice – say five out of seven and the like – then it is essential to read all the questions so you can eliminate the two that are most difficult. If, however, you are asked to answer all the questions, there may be danger in trying to answer the easiest one first because you may find that you will spend too much time on it. The best technique is to answer the first question, then proceed to the second, etc.

5) Time your answers. Before the exam begins, write down the time it started, then add the time allowed for the examination and write down the time it must be completed, then divide the time available somewhat as follows:
   - If 3-1/2 hours are allowed, that would be 210 minutes. If you have 80 objective-type questions, that would be an average of 2-1/2 minutes per question. Allow yourself no more than 2 minutes per question, or a total of 160 minutes, which will permit about 50 minutes to review.
   - If for the time allotment of 210 minutes there are 7 essay questions to answer, that would average about 30 minutes a question. Give yourself only 25 minutes per question so that you have about 35 minutes to review.

6) The most important instruction is to *read each question* and make sure you know what is wanted. The second most important instruction is to *time yourself properly* so that you answer every question. The third most important instruction is to *answer every question*. Guess if you have to but include something for each question. Remember that you will receive no credit for a blank and will probably receive some credit if you write something in answer to an essay question. If you guess a letter – say "B" for a multiple-choice question – you may have guessed right. If you leave a blank as an answer to a multiple-choice question, the examiners may respect your feelings but it will not add a point to your score. Some exams may penalize you for wrong answers, so in such cases *only*, you may not want to guess unless you have some basis for your answer.

7) Suggestions
   a. Objective-type questions
      1. Examine the question booklet for proper sequence of pages and questions
      2. Read all instructions carefully
      3. Skip any question which seems too difficult; return to it after all other questions have been answered
      4. Apportion your time properly; do not spend too much time on any single question or group of questions

5. Note and underline key words – *all, most, fewest, least, best, worst, same, opposite,* etc.
6. Pay particular attention to negatives
7. Note unusual option, e.g., unduly long, short, complex, different or similar in content to the body of the question
8. Observe the use of "hedging" words – *probably, may, most likely,* etc.
9. Make sure that your answer is put next to the same number as the question
10. Do not second-guess unless you have good reason to believe the second answer is definitely more correct
11. Cross out original answer if you decide another answer is more accurate; do not erase until you are ready to hand your paper in
12. Answer all questions; guess unless instructed otherwise
13. Leave time for review

b. Essay questions
   1. Read each question carefully
   2. Determine exactly what is wanted. Underline key words or phrases.
   3. Decide on outline or paragraph answer
   4. Include many different points and elements unless asked to develop any one or two points or elements
   5. Show impartiality by giving pros and cons unless directed to select one side only
   6. Make and write down any assumptions you find necessary to answer the questions
   7. Watch your English, grammar, punctuation and choice of words
   8. Time your answers; don't crowd material

8) Answering the essay question

Most essay questions can be answered by framing the specific response around several key words or ideas. Here are a few such key words or ideas:

M's: manpower, materials, methods, money, management
P's: purpose, program, policy, plan, procedure, practice, problems, pitfalls, personnel, public relations
   a. Six basic steps in handling problems:
      1. Preliminary plan and background development
      2. Collect information, data and facts
      3. Analyze and interpret information, data and facts
      4. Analyze and develop solutions as well as make recommendations
      5. Prepare report and sell recommendations
      6. Install recommendations and follow up effectiveness

   b. Pitfalls to avoid
      1. *Taking things for granted* – A statement of the situation does not necessarily imply that each of the elements is necessarily true; for example, a complaint may be invalid and biased so that all that can be taken for granted is that a complaint has been registered

2. *Considering only one side of a situation* – Wherever possible, indicate several alternatives and then point out the reasons you selected the best one
3. *Failing to indicate follow up* – Whenever your answer indicates action on your part, make certain that you will take proper follow-up action to see how successful your recommendations, procedures or actions turn out to be
4. *Taking too long in answering any single question* – Remember to time your answers properly

IX. AFTER THE TEST

Scoring procedures differ in detail among civil service jurisdictions although the general principles are the same. Whether the papers are hand-scored or graded by machine we have described, they are nearly always graded by number. That is, the person who marks the paper knows only the number – never the name – of the applicant. Not until all the papers have been graded will they be matched with names. If other tests, such as training and experience or oral interview ratings have been given, scores will be combined. Different parts of the examination usually have different weights. For example, the written test might count 60 percent of the final grade, and a rating of training and experience 40 percent. In many jurisdictions, veterans will have a certain number of points added to their grades.

After the final grade has been determined, the names are placed in grade order and an eligible list is established. There are various methods for resolving ties between those who get the same final grade – probably the most common is to place first the name of the person whose application was received first. Job offers are made from the eligible list in the order the names appear on it. You will be notified of your grade and your rank as soon as all these computations have been made. This will be done as rapidly as possible.

People who are found to meet the requirements in the announcement are called "eligibles." Their names are put on a list of eligible candidates. An eligible's chances of getting a job depend on how high he stands on this list and how fast agencies are filling jobs from the list.

When a job is to be filled from a list of eligibles, the agency asks for the names of people on the list of eligibles for that job. When the civil service commission receives this request, it sends to the agency the names of the three people highest on this list. Or, if the job to be filled has specialized requirements, the office sends the agency the names of the top three persons who meet these requirements from the general list.

The appointing officer makes a choice from among the three people whose names were sent to him. If the selected person accepts the appointment, the names of the others are put back on the list to be considered for future openings.

That is the rule in hiring from all kinds of eligible lists, whether they are for typist, carpenter, chemist, or something else. For every vacancy, the appointing officer has his choice of any one of the top three eligibles on the list. This explains why the person whose name is on top of the list sometimes does not get an appointment when some of the persons lower on the list do. If the appointing officer chooses the second or third eligible, the No. 1 eligible does not get a job at once, but stays on the list until he is appointed or the list is terminated.

X. HOW TO PASS THE INTERVIEW TEST

The examination for which you applied requires an oral interview test. You have already taken the written test and you are now being called for the interview test – the final part of the formal examination.

You may think that it is not possible to prepare for an interview test and that there are no procedures to follow during an interview. Our purpose is to point out some things you can do in advance that will help you and some good rules to follow and pitfalls to avoid while you are being interviewed.

What is an interview supposed to test?

The written examination is designed to test the technical knowledge and competence of the candidate; the oral is designed to evaluate intangible qualities, not readily measured otherwise, and to establish a list showing the relative fitness of each candidate – as measured against his competitors – for the position sought. Scoring is not on the basis of "right" and "wrong," but on a sliding scale of values ranging from "not passable" to "outstanding." As a matter of fact, it is possible to achieve a relatively low score without a single "incorrect" answer because of evident weakness in the qualities being measured.

Occasionally, an examination may consist entirely of an oral test – either an individual or a group oral. In such cases, information is sought concerning the technical knowledges and abilities of the candidate, since there has been no written examination for this purpose. More commonly, however, an oral test is used to supplement a written examination.

Who conducts interviews?

The composition of oral boards varies among different jurisdictions. In nearly all, a representative of the personnel department serves as chairman. One of the members of the board may be a representative of the department in which the candidate would work. In some cases, "outside experts" are used, and, frequently, a businessman or some other representative of the general public is asked to serve. Labor and management or other special groups may be represented. The aim is to secure the services of experts in the appropriate field.

However the board is composed, it is a good idea (and not at all improper or unethical) to ascertain in advance of the interview who the members are and what groups they represent. When you are introduced to them, you will have some idea of their backgrounds and interests, and at least you will not stutter and stammer over their names.

What should be done before the interview?

While knowledge about the board members is useful and takes some of the surprise element out of the interview, there is other preparation which is more substantive. It *is* possible to prepare for an oral interview – in several ways:

1) Keep a copy of your application and review it carefully before the interview

This may be the only document before the oral board, and the starting point of the interview. Know what education and experience you have listed there, and the sequence and dates of all of it. Sometimes the board will ask you to review the highlights of your experience for them; you should not have to hem and haw doing it.

2) Study the class specification and the examination announcement

Usually, the oral board has one or both of these to guide them. The qualities, characteristics or knowledges required by the position sought are stated in these documents. They offer valuable clues as to the nature of the oral interview. For example, if the job involves supervisory responsibilities, the announcement will usually indicate that knowledge of modern supervisory methods and the qualifications of the candidate as a supervisor will be tested. If so, you can expect such questions, frequently in the form of a hypothetical situation which you are expected to solve. NEVER go into an oral without knowledge of the duties and responsibilities of the job you seek.

3) Think through each qualification required

Try to visualize the kind of questions you would ask if you were a board member. How well could you answer them? Try especially to appraise your own knowledge and background in each area, *measured against the job sought*, and identify any areas in which you are weak. Be critical and realistic – do not flatter yourself.

4) Do some general reading in areas in which you feel you may be weak

For example, if the job involves supervision and your past experience has NOT, some general reading in supervisory methods and practices, particularly in the field of human relations, might be useful. Do NOT study agency procedures or detailed manuals. The oral board will be testing your understanding and capacity, not your memory.

5) Get a good night's sleep and watch your general health and mental attitude

You will want a clear head at the interview. Take care of a cold or any other minor ailment, and of course, no hangovers.

What should be done on the day of the interview?

Now comes the day of the interview itself. Give yourself plenty of time to get there. Plan to arrive somewhat ahead of the scheduled time, particularly if your appointment is in the fore part of the day. If a previous candidate fails to appear, the board might be ready for you a bit early. By early afternoon an oral board is almost invariably behind schedule if there are many candidates, and you may have to wait. Take along a book or magazine to read, or your application to review, but leave any extraneous material in the waiting room when you go in for your interview. In any event, relax and compose yourself.

The matter of dress is important. The board is forming impressions about you – from your experience, your manners, your attitude, and your appearance. Give your personal appearance careful attention. Dress your best, but not your flashiest. Choose conservative, appropriate clothing, and be sure it is immaculate. This is a business interview, and your appearance should indicate that you regard it as such. Besides, being well groomed and properly dressed will help boost your confidence.

Sooner or later, someone will call your name and escort you into the interview room. *This is it.* From here on you are on your own. It is too late for any more preparation. But remember, you asked for this opportunity to prove your fitness, and you are here because your request was granted.

What happens when you go in?

The usual sequence of events will be as follows: The clerk (who is often the board stenographer) will introduce you to the chairman of the oral board, who will introduce you to the other members of the board. Acknowledge the introductions before you sit down. Do not be surprised if you find a microphone facing you or a stenotypist sitting by. Oral interviews are usually recorded in the event of an appeal or other review.

Usually the chairman of the board will open the interview by reviewing the highlights of your education and work experience from your application – primarily for the benefit of the other members of the board, as well as to get the material into the record. Do not interrupt or comment unless there is an error or significant misinterpretation; if that is the case, do not hesitate. But do not quibble about insignificant matters. Also, he will usually ask you some question about your education, experience or your present job – partly to get you to start talking and to establish the interviewing "rapport." He may start the actual questioning, or turn it over to one of the other members. Frequently, each member undertakes the questioning on a particular area, one in which he is perhaps most competent, so you can expect each member to participate in the examination. Because time is limited, you may also expect some rather abrupt switches in the direction the questioning takes, so do not be upset by it. Normally, a board member will not pursue a single line of questioning unless he discovers a particular strength or weakness.

After each member has participated, the chairman will usually ask whether any member has any further questions, then will ask you if you have anything you wish to add. Unless you are expecting this question, it may floor you. Worse, it may start you off on an extended, extemporaneous speech. The board is not usually seeking more information. The question is principally to offer you a last opportunity to present further qualifications or to indicate that you have nothing to add. So, if you feel that a significant qualification or characteristic has been overlooked, it is proper to point it out in a sentence or so. Do not compliment the board on the thoroughness of their examination – they have been sketchy, and you know it. If you wish, merely say, "No thank you, I have nothing further to add." This is a point where you can "talk yourself out" of a good impression or fail to present an important bit of information. Remember, *you close the interview yourself*.

The chairman will then say, "That is all, Mr. _____, thank you." Do not be startled; the interview is over, and quicker than you think. Thank him, gather your belongings and take your leave. Save your sigh of relief for the other side of the door.

How to put your best foot forward

Throughout this entire process, you may feel that the board individually and collectively is trying to pierce your defenses, seek out your hidden weaknesses and embarrass and confuse you. Actually, this is not true. They are obliged to make an appraisal of your qualifications for the job you are seeking, and they want to see you in your best light. Remember, they must interview all candidates and a non-cooperative candidate may become a failure in spite of their best efforts to bring out his qualifications. Here are 15 suggestions that will help you:

1) Be natural – Keep your attitude confident, not cocky

If you are not confident that you can do the job, do not expect the board to be. Do not apologize for your weaknesses, try to bring out your strong points. The board is interested in a positive, not negative, presentation. Cockiness will antagonize any board member and make him wonder if you are covering up a weakness by a false show of strength.

2) Get comfortable, but don't lounge or sprawl

Sit erectly but not stiffly. A careless posture may lead the board to conclude that you are careless in other things, or at least that you are not impressed by the importance of the occasion. Either conclusion is natural, even if incorrect. Do not fuss with your clothing, a pencil or an ashtray. Your hands may occasionally be useful to emphasize a point; do not let them become a point of distraction.

3) Do not wisecrack or make small talk

This is a serious situation, and your attitude should show that you consider it as such. Further, the time of the board is limited – they do not want to waste it, and neither should you.

4) Do not exaggerate your experience or abilities

In the first place, from information in the application or other interviews and sources, the board may know more about you than you think. Secondly, you probably will not get away with it. An experienced board is rather adept at spotting such a situation, so do not take the chance.

5) If you know a board member, do not make a point of it, yet do not hide it

Certainly you are not fooling him, and probably not the other members of the board. Do not try to take advantage of your acquaintanceship – it will probably do you little good.

6) Do not dominate the interview

Let the board do that. They will give you the clues – do not assume that you have to do all the talking. Realize that the board has a number of questions to ask you, and do not try to take up all the interview time by showing off your extensive knowledge of the answer to the first one.

7) Be attentive

You only have 20 minutes or so, and you should keep your attention at its sharpest throughout. When a member is addressing a problem or question to you, give him your undivided attention. Address your reply principally to him, but do not exclude the other board members.

8) Do not interrupt

A board member may be stating a problem for you to analyze. He will ask you a question when the time comes. Let him state the problem, and wait for the question.

9) Make sure you understand the question

Do not try to answer until you are sure what the question is. If it is not clear, restate it in your own words or ask the board member to clarify it for you. However, do not haggle about minor elements.

10) Reply promptly but not hastily

A common entry on oral board rating sheets is "candidate responded readily," or "candidate hesitated in replies." Respond as promptly and quickly as you can, but do not jump to a hasty, ill-considered answer.

11) Do not be peremptory in your answers

A brief answer is proper – but do not fire your answer back. That is a losing game from your point of view. The board member can probably ask questions much faster than you can answer them.

12) Do not try to create the answer you think the board member wants

He is interested in what kind of mind you have and how it works – not in playing games. Furthermore, he can usually spot this practice and will actually grade you down on it.

13) Do not switch sides in your reply merely to agree with a board member

Frequently, a member will take a contrary position merely to draw you out and to see if you are willing and able to defend your point of view. Do not start a debate, yet do not surrender a good position. If a position is worth taking, it is worth defending.

14) Do not be afraid to admit an error in judgment if you are shown to be wrong

The board knows that you are forced to reply without any opportunity for careful consideration. Your answer may be demonstrably wrong. If so, admit it and get on with the interview.

15) Do not dwell at length on your present job

The opening question may relate to your present assignment. Answer the question but do not go into an extended discussion. You are being examined for a *new* job, not your present one. As a matter of fact, try to phrase ALL your answers in terms of the job for which you are being examined.

Basis of Rating

Probably you will forget most of these "do's" and "don'ts" when you walk into the oral interview room. Even remembering them all will not ensure you a passing grade. Perhaps you did not have the qualifications in the first place. But remembering them will help you to put your best foot forward, without treading on the toes of the board members.

Rumor and popular opinion to the contrary notwithstanding, an oral board wants you to make the best appearance possible. They know you are under pressure – but they also want to see how you respond to it as a guide to what your reaction would be under the pressures of the job you seek. They will be influenced by the degree of poise you display, the personal traits you show and the manner in which you respond.

ABOUT THIS BOOK

This book contains tests divided into Examination Sections. Go through each test, answering every question in the margin. We have also attached a sample answer sheet at the back of the book that can be removed and used. At the end of each test look at the answer key and check your answers. On the ones you got wrong, look at the right answer choice and learn. Do not fill in the answers first. Do not memorize the questions and answers, but understand the answer and principles involved. On your test, the questions will likely be different from the samples. Questions are changed and new ones added. If you understand these past questions you should have success with any changes that arise. Tests may consist of several types of questions. We have additional books on each subject should more study be advisable or necessary for you. Finally, the more you study, the better prepared you will be. This book is intended to be the last thing you study before you walk into the examination room. Prior study of relevant texts is also recommended. NLC publishes some of these in our Fundamental Series. Knowledge and good sense are important factors in passing your exam. Good luck also helps. So now study this Passbook, absorb the material contained within and take that knowledge into the examination. Then do your best to pass that exam.

EXAMINATION SECTION

EXAMINATION SECTION
TEST 1

DIRECTIONS: Each question or incomplete statement is followed by several suggested answers or completions. Select the one that BEST answers the question or completes the statement. *PRINT THE LETTER OF THE CORRECT ANSWER IN THE SPACE AT THE RIGHT.*

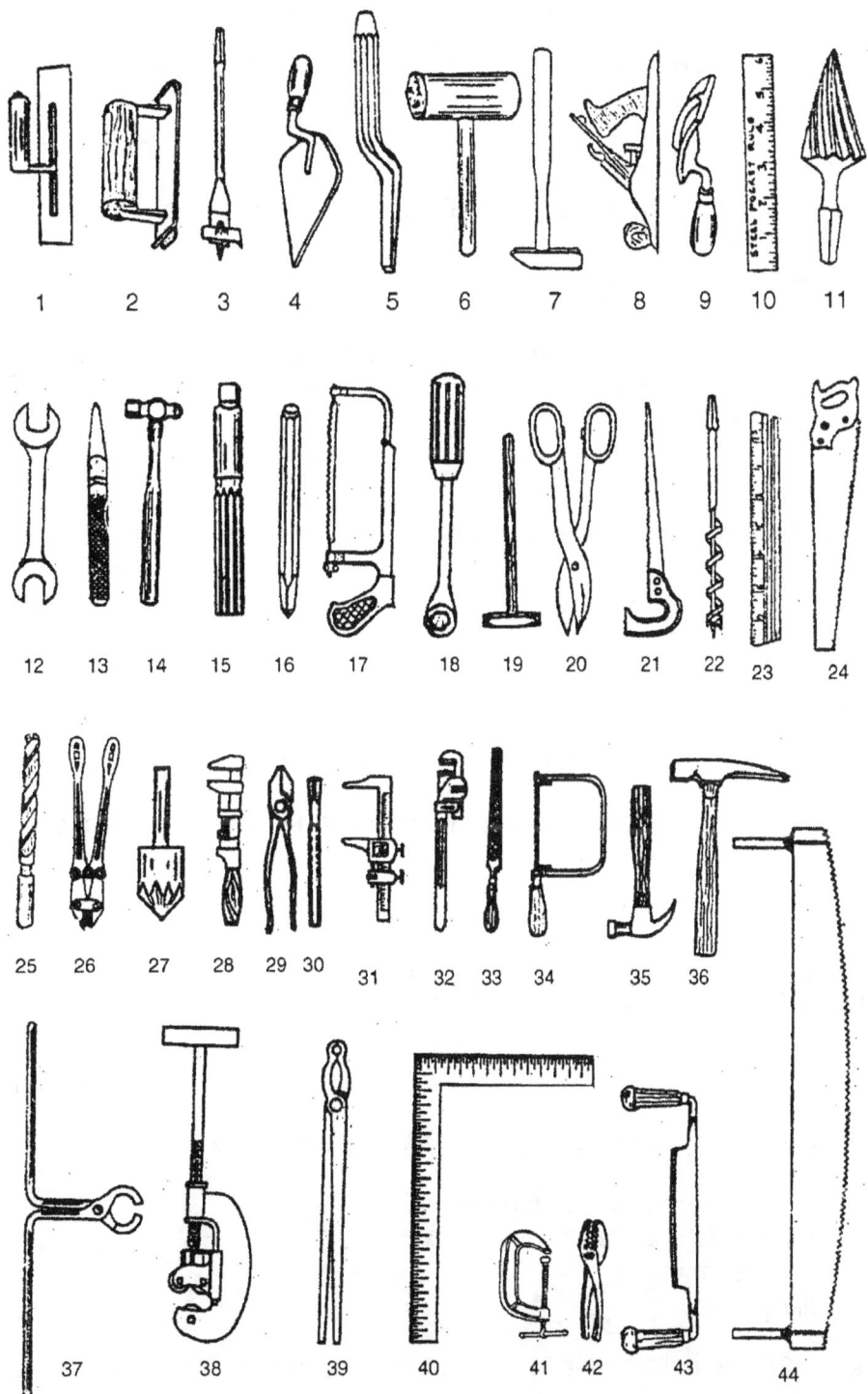

1

1. Of the following, which group of three tools is used *most nearly* in the same way? 1.____

   A. Tools 4, 21, 39 B. Tools 11, 16, 42
   C. Tools 14, 35, 36 D. Tools 5, 6, 13

2. If you want to cut a disc out of sheet metal, you should use tool no. 2.____

   A. 20 B. 26 C. 29 D. 38

3. Tool number 25 is ordinarily NOT used alone; it should be used with tool no. 3.____

   A. 28 B. 35
   C. 39 D. another tool not pictured

4. To split a brick in half you should FIRST chip the line of division all the way around the brick with tool no. 4.____

   A. 14 B. 24 C. 34 D. 36

5. To repair wide cracks in a wood floor you should glue a thin strip of wood into the crack and then level it even with the surrounding floor surface. To level this strip of wood you should use tool no. 5.____

   A. 1 B. 8 C. 24 D. 33

6. To smooth a newly laid concrete surface so that it is free of ripples and marks, you should use tool no. 6.____

   A. 1 B. 6 C. 8 D. 9

7. To measure the *outside* diameter of a section of pipe MOST accurately, the tool that should be used is tool no. 7.____

   A. 10 B. 23 C. 31 D. 40

8. The BEST tool to use to cut a curved pattern in a 1/4 inch-thick sheet of plywood is tool no. 8.____

   A. 17 B. 24 C. 34 D. 43

9. If you, as a member of a repair crew, plan to cut a rectangular piece of plywood measuring 18" x 12" out of a larger rectangular piece measuring 30" x 24", the tool that will BEST help lay out the lines and check the angles is number 9.____

   A. 10 B. 23 C. 31 D. 40

10. Either end of tool 12 can be *properly* used for the purpose of 10.____

    A. fitting into the handle of another tool
    B. turning nuts or bolts
    C. laying out angles
    D. pulling nails

11. Tools 22, 24, 35 and 40 have in common that fact that they are used *primarily* in 11.____

    A. masonry B. plumbing
    C. sheet metal work D. woodworking

12. Which tool requires the use of BOTH hands on the tool to operate it properly? 12.____
    A. Tool 8　　B. Tool 12　　C. Tool 20　　D. Tool 24

13. Of the following, the tool designed to be used for turning nuts of various sizes is tool no. 13.____
    A. 19　　B. 28　　C. 29　　D. 31

14. To cut a section of pipe to the required length, the MOST appropriate tool is number 14.____
    A. 20　　B. 29　　C. 31　　D. 38

15. In the picture below of a roof, which one of the numbered arrows points to the "flashing"? 15.____
    A. 1　　B. 2　　C. 3　　D. 4

16. The function of glazier's points is to 16.____

    A. keep the putty from dirtying the glass
    B. make it easy to cut glass in a straight line
    C. hold a pane of glass in place
    D. aid in applying putty evenly around the glass

17. It is *desirable* for a putty knife used for patching plaster cracks to be flexible because a flexible putty knife 17.____

    A. makes it difficult for the user to cut his hands while applying the plaster
    B. is easier to keep clean than one made of rigid material
    C. can press the patching materials into the crack, filling it completely
    D. makes it possible to pick up the exact amount of plaster required

18. Using a fuse with a *larger* rated capacity than that of the circuit is 18.____

    A. *advisable;* such use prevents the fuse from blowing
    B. *advisable;* larger capacity fuses last longer than smaller capacity fuses
    C. *inadvisable;* larger capacity fuses are more expensive than smaller capacity fuses
    D. *inadvisable;* such use may cause a fire

19. You can MOST easily tell when a screw-in type fuse has blown because the center of the strip of metal in the fuse is 19.____

    A. broken　　　　　　　　　B. visible
    C. nicked　　　　　　　　　D. cool to the touch

20. In the picture below, which of the numbered arrows points to the door "jamb"? 20._____

    A. 1   B. 2   C. 3   D. 4

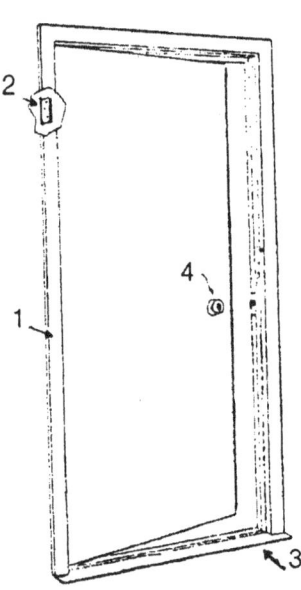

21. Of the following, the MAIN reason why flashing is used in the building trade is to make an area 21._____

    A. decorative   B. watertight   C. level   D. heat-resistant

22. To prepare a ready-mixed concrete material for use, you FIRST add 22._____

    A. gravel   B. salt   C. sand   D. water

23. When working on wet floors with an electrically powered tool, additional safety against electric shock can BEST be provided by 23._____

    A. a longer electric cord
    C. rubber gloves
    B. an AC-DC converter
    D. loose clothing

24. Which one of the wrenches pictured below is designed to grip round pipes in making plumbing repairs? 24._____

    A. 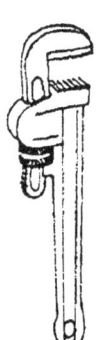   B.    C.    D.

25. Which one of the saws pictured below would be BEST to use to cut steel bar stock?   25.____

    A.   B.

    C.   D.

26. Which one of the hammers pictured below is a claw hammer?   26.____

    A.   B.   C.   D.

27. The terms "dovetail" and "dowel" are used to describe types of   27.____

    A. glues   B. joints   C. clamps   D. tile

28. A three-prong plug on a power tool used on a 120-volt line indicates that the tool   28.____

    A. may be grounded against electric shock
    B. is provided with additional power through the third prong
    C. has a defect and should be returned
    D. is adaptable for use with AC or DC current

29. A bit and brace should be used to   29.____

    A. saw wood   B. glue wood
    C. drill holes   D. support or hold work

30. Which of the following would ordinarily occur FIRST in a toilet tank after the handle is pushed down to flush the toilet?   30.____

    A. Float ball drops with water level, opening the ballcock assembly through which fresh water flows into the tank
    B. Tank ball sinks slowly into place
    C. Rising water pushes the float ball up until it closes the ballcock assembly, shutting off the supply of fresh water when the tank is full
    D. The tank ball lifts, opening the outlet so water can flow from tank to bowl

KEY (CORRECT ANSWERS)

1. C
2. A
3. D
4. D
5. B

6. A
7. C
8. C
9. D
10. B

11. D
12. A
13. B
14. D
15. B

16. C
17. C
18. D
19. A
20. A

21. B
22. D
23. C
24. A
25. B

26. C
27. B
28. A
29. C
30. D

TEST 2

DIRECTIONS: Each question or incomplete statement is followed by several suggested answers or completions. Select the one that BEST answers the question or completes the statement. *PRINT THE LETTER OF THE CORRECT ANSWER IN THE SPACE AT THE RIGHT.*

1. Of the following, the MAIN reason for clear glass doors to have a painted design about four and one-half feet above the floor is to   1.____

    A. look attractive
    B. prevent glare
    C. improve safety
    D. make damage, if any, less noticeable

2. When using a wrench to make a repair on a faucet, it is a good idea to cover the wrench with rags in order to   2.____

    A. protect the finish on the faucet
    B. get a closer fit over the faucet
    C. get a better grip on the wrench
    D. get a better grip on the faucet

3. The length of the screw in the sketch below is *most nearly*   3.____

    A. 1 7/8"   B. 2"   C. 2 1/4"   D. 2 5/16"

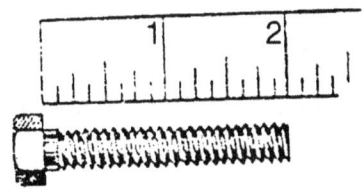

4. Panel doors may have horns which must be cut off before the door is hung. In the sketch below, the arrow which indicates a horn is labeled number   4.____

    A. 1   B. 2   C. 3   D. 4

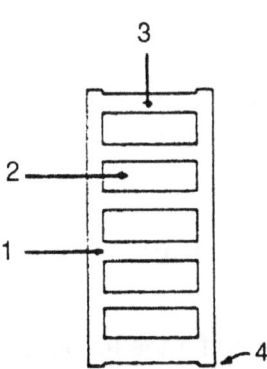

7

5. To "shim a hinge" means to

   A. swing the hinge from side to side
   B. paint the hinge
   C. polish the hinge
   D. raise up the hinge

6. To hold work that is being planed, sawed, drilled, shaped, sharpened or riveted, you should use a

   A. punch   B. rasp   C. reamer   D. vise

7. A good deal of the trouble caused by faulty and worn locks and hinges can be avoided by proper lubrication.
   The tool you would use to lubricate locks and hinges is

   A. [hose clamp]   B. [oil can]   C. [putty knife]   D. [paint brush]

8. The terms ALLIGATORING, BLISTERING, and PEELING refer to

   A. carpentry   B. masonry   C. painting   D. plumbing

9. The terms BAT and STRETCHER refer to

   A. carpentry   B. glazing   C. masonry   D. painting

10. Ladders which are used to extend as high as 60 feet are called

    A. extension ladders   B. portable ladders
    C. single-section ladders   D. stepladders

11. Of the following, the MOST important advantage that Plexiglass has over regular glass, when used in windows, is that it

    A. is available in a wide range of thicknesses
    B. is easier to clean
    C. offers greater resistance to breakage
    D. offers greater resistance to scratches

12. Clutch-head, offset, Phillips and spiral-ratchet all are different types of

    A. drills   B. files   C. wrenches   D. screwdrivers

13. Of the following, the MOST important reason for keeping tools in perfect working order is to make sure

    A. the proper tool is being used for the required work
    B. the tools can be operated safely
    C. each employee can repair a variety of building defects
    D. no employee uses a tool for his private use

14. When repairing a hole in a leaking pipe which of the following should be done FIRST?   14.____

    A. Wrap tape around the hole
    B. Turn off the water supply
    C. Tighten a clamp around the hole
    D. Seal the hole with epoxy

15. Freshly cut threads on pipe should be handled with caution *mainly* because the threads   15.____

    A. are the weakest section of the pipe and break easily
    B. do not give a firm handhold for carrying
    C. make a tight seal around a joint
    D. are always sharp

16. When a repair worker must enter a confined space through a small opening, it is a GOOD idea to attach a rope to his body *mainly* because the   16.____

    A. rope reduces unnecessary strain on the body
    B. rope may provide a way to reach the worker in an emergency
    C. worker will be able to get to areas that are not easily reached
    D. worker may be able to use the rope to remove debris from the work space

17. Hitting the handle of a screw driver with a hammer to remove an imbedded screw is a   17.____

    A. *good* practice, since it supplies the necessary force to get the screw started
    B. *poor* practice, since the shank part of the screw driver can be bent and the tool made useless
    C. *good* practice, since hammers and screw drivers are available in every tool kit just for this purpose
    D. *poor* practice, since the blade tip of the screw driver cannot be guided into the screw slot when both hands are holding the tools

18. Of the following, the reason why a tank, such as that pictured below, that is otherwise working correctly might fail to fill up sufficiently to deliver enough water to the toilet bowl at the time it is needed is that the   18.____

    A. ball may not drop back over the valve seat
    B. excess water may be flowing into the drain
    C. float rod may be bent up
    D. valve seat may be worn or nicked

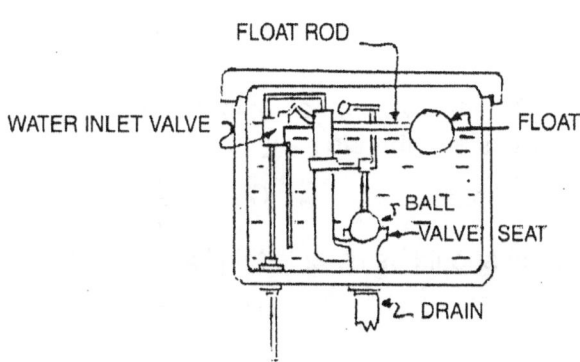

19. In the sketch below, the measurement of the inside diameter is *most nearly* _____ inches.

   A. 24   B. 3   C. 3 1/2   D. 4

20. In a two-wire electrical system, the color of the wire which is grounded is *usually*

   A. white   B. red   C. black   D. green

21. It is generally recommended that wooden ladders be kept coated with a suitable protective coating.
   The one of the following which is NOT a suitable protective coating is

   A. clear lacquer   B. clear varnish
   C. linseed oil   D. paint

22. The tool you should use to mend metal by soldering is

   A.   B.   C.   D.

23. Of the following, the MOST effective method of fixing a door that sticks is to locate the area of the door which sticks and then to _____ it.

   A. lacquer   B. plane   C. tape   D. varnish

24. Which one of the following should be used to thin latex paint?

   A. Mineral spirits   B. Turpentine
   C. Denatured alcohol   D. Water

25. Of the following, the MAIN reason you should NOT place a ladder directly in front of a door that opens toward the ladder is that

    A. there is not enough space to support the weight of the ladder
    B. you would have to step down off the ladder each time someone wants to use the door
    C. this would prove to be hazardous if someone comes through the door
    D. it would be hard to reach the areas that need repair without tipping the ladder off balance

26. Going over the cutting line MORE than once when cutting a pane of glass by hand with a cutting wheel is *usually*

    A. *advisable;* it gives a straighter line
    B. *advisable;* it gives a cleaner break
    C. *inadvisable;* it gives an uneven break
    D. *inadvisable;* it may blunt the edge of the glass cutter

27. When hammering, it is usually BEST to hold the handle of the hammer

    A. close to the head because this maximizes the force of the blow
    B. far away from the head because this maximizes the force of the blow
    C. close to the head because this reduces the force of the blow
    D. far away from the head because this reduces the force of the blow

28. Repair crew members should report accidents on the job IMMEDIATELY *primarily* so that

    A. the proper person will be reprimanded for his carelessness
    B. a correct count can be kept of time lost through accidents
    C. prompt medical care may be given when needed
    D. the correct forms will be filled out

29. Leather gloves should be worn when handling sheet metal *primarily* because

    A. pressure on the metal might cause it to bend
    B. the edges and corners of the metal may be sharp
    C. natural oil or moisture from hands corrodes the metal
    D. leather provides a more secure grip

30. If a portable ladder does NOT have a nonslip base, the way to overcome this deficiency so that the ladder can be used safely is to

    A. place the ladder on soft earth
    B. fasten a wooden board across the top of the ladder
    C. splice two short ladders together
    D. tie the bottom of the ladder to a secure structure

KEY (CORRECT ANSWERS)

1.	C	16.	B
2.	A	17.	B
3.	B	18.	A
4.	D	19.	B
5.	D	20.	A
6.	D	21.	D
7.	B	22.	B
8.	C	23.	B
9.	C	24.	D
10.	A	25.	C
11.	C	26.	C
12.	D	27.	B
13.	B	28.	C
14.	B	29.	B
15.	D	30.	D

EXAMINATION SECTION
TEST 1

DIRECTIONS: Each question or incomplete statement is followed by several suggested answers or completions. Select the one that BEST answers the question or completes the statement. *PRINT THE LETTER OF THE CORRECT ANSWEE IN THE SPACE AT THE RIGHT.*

1. As a member of a repair crew, you have been asked by your supervisor to reinforce a door. You have never done this kind of work before and are not certain how to go about it. Of the following, the MOST advisable action to take is to

    A. tell your supervisor you need assistance
    B. ask the other crew members if they can help you
    C. go ahead and do the best you can
    D. ask another member of your crew if he will do it for you

    1._____

2. It is BEST to erect a barricade or barrier before repair work begins *mainly* because

    A. the repair truck can be sent back for additional supplies
    B. the workers can work in more comfortable space
    C. unauthorized persons are kept clear of the work area
    D. a solid platform is provided for workers' use

    2._____

3. Of the following, the BEST reason for sprinkling water on work areas which have a lot of dust or where the work itself will create a lot of dust is that this action will

    A. dissolve the dust particles
    B. help the dust to settle
    C. clean away the dust from the area
    D. prevent the dust from drying out

    3._____

QUESTIONS 4-9.
Questions 4 through 9 are to be answered *solely* on the basis of the following set of instructions.

Patching Simple Cracks in a Built-Up Roof

If there is a visible crack in built-up roofing, the repair is simple and straight forward:
1. With a brush, clean all loose gravel and dust out of the crack, and clean three or four inches around all sides of it.
2. With a trowel or putty knife, fill the crack with asphalt cement and then spread a layer of asphalt cement about 1/8 inch thick over the cleaned area.
3. Place a strip of roofing felt big enough to cover the crack into the wet cement and press it down firmly.
4. Spread a second layer of cement over the strip of felt and well past its edges.
5. Brush gravel back over the patch.

4. According to the above passage, in order to patch simple cracks in a built-up roof, it is necessary to use a

    A. putty knife and a drill   B. knife and pliers
    C. tack hammer and a punch   D. brush and a trowe

    4._____

5. According to the above passage, the size of the area that should be clear of loose gravel and dust before the asphalt cement is first applied should

   A. be the exact size of the crack itself
   B. extend three or four inches on all sides of the crack
   C. be 1/8 inch greater than the size of the crack itself
   D. extend the length of the roofing strip

5.____

6. According to the above passage, loose gravel and dust in the crack should be removed with a

   A. brush   B. felt pad   C. trowel   D. dust mop

6.____

7. Assume that both layers of asphalt cement needed to patch the crack are of the same thickness.
   The total thickness of asphalt cement used in the patch should be, *most nearly,* _____ inch.

   A. 1/2   B. 1/3   C. 1/4   D. 1/8

7.____

8. According to the instructions in the above passage, how large should the strip of roofing felt be cut?

   A. Three of four inches square
   B. Smaller than the crack and small enough to be surrounded by cement on all sides of the strip
   C. Exactly the same size and shape of the area covered by the wet cement
   D. Large enough to completely cover the crack

8.____

9. The final or finishing action to be taken in patching a simple crack in a built-up roof is to

   A. clean out the inside of the crack
   B. spread a layer of asphalt a second time
   C. cover the crack with roofing felt
   D. cover the patch of roofing felt and cement with gravel

9.____

10. As a repair crew worker, your supervisor tells you that he has in the workshop a piece of glass measuring 5' x 4' from which he wants you to cut a section measuring 4'8" x 3'2". However, you find two pieces of glass in the workshop; one is 5' x 3', and the other is 8' x 5'.
    Of the following, the BEST action for you to take is to

    A. cut a section measuring 4'8" x 3' from the smaller piece because that is probably what he meant
    B. do NOT cut the glass and wait until he asks you for it
    C. tell him about the differences in measurement and ask him what to do
    D. cut a section measuring 4'8" x 3'2" from the larger piece since that would give you the full size required

10.____

11. A floor that is 9' wide by 12' long measures how many square feet?

    A. 12   B. 21   C. 108   D. 150

11.____

12. The sum of 5 1/16, 4 1/4, 4 3/8, and 3 7/16 is   12.____

    A. 17 1/8   B. 17 7/16   C. 17 1/4   D. 17 3/8

13. From a length of pipe 6 feet 9 inches long you are asked to cut a piece 4 feet 5 inches   13.____
    long.
    The length of the remainder, in inches, should be

    A. 24   B. 26   C. 28   D. 53

QUESTIONS 14-17.
In answering questions 14 through 17 refer to the label pictured below.

LABEL

BREGSON'S CLEAR GLUE HIGHLY FLAMMABLE	PRECAUTIONS
A clear quick-drying glue	Use with adequate ventilation
For temporary bonding, apply glue to one surface and join immediately	Close container after use
For permanent bonding, apply glue to both surfaces, permit to dry and press together	Keep out of reach of children
Use for bonding plastic to plastic, plastic to wood, and wood to wood only	Avoid prolonged breathing of vapors and repeated contact with skin
Will not bond at temperatures below 60°	

14. Assume that you, as a member of a repair crew, have been asked to repair a wood ban-   14.____
    ister in the hallway of a house. Since the heat has been turned off, the hallway is very
    cold, except for the location where you have to make the repair. Another repair crew
    worker is working at that same location using a blow torch to solder a pipe in the wall.

    The temperature at that location is about 67°.
    According to the instruction on the above label, the use of this glue to make the neces-
    sary repair is

    A. *advisable;* the glue will bond wood to wood
    B. *advisable;* the heat form the soldering will cause the glue to dry quickly
    C. *inadvisable;* the work area temperature is too low
    D. *inadvisable;* the glue is highly flammable

15. According to the instructions on the above label, this glue should NOT be used for which   15.____
    of the following applications?

    A. Affixing a pine table leg to a walnut table
    B. Repairing leaks around pipe joints
    C. Bonding a plastic knob to a cedar drawer
    D. Attaching a lucite knob to a lucite drawer

16. According to the instructions on the above label, using this glue to bond ceramic tile to a plaster wall by coating both surfaces with glue, letting the glue dry, and then pressing the tile to the plaster wall is   16.____

   A. *advisable;* the glue is quick drying and clear
   B. *advisable;* the glue should be permanently affixed to the one surface of the tile only
   C. *inadvisable;* the glue is not suitable for bonding ceramic tile to plaster walls
   D. *inadvisable;* the bonding should be a temporary one

17. The precaution described in the above label "use with adequate ventilation" means that   17.____

   A. the area you are working in should be very cold
   B. there should be sufficient fresh air where you are using the glue
   C. you should wear gloves to avoid contact with the glue
   D. you must apply a lot of glue to make a permanent bond

QUESTIONS 18-20.
Questions 18 through 20 are to be answered *solely* on the basis of the following passage.

   A utility plan is a floor plan which shows the layout of a heating, electrical, plumbing, or other utility system. Utility plans are used primarily by the persons responsible for the utilities, but they are important to the craftsman as well. Most utility installations require the leaving of openings in walls, floors, and roofs for the admission or installation of utility features. The craftsman who is, for example, pouring a concrete foundation wall must study the utility plans to determine the number, sizes, and locations of the openings he must leave for piping, electric lines, and the like.

18. The one of the following items of information which is LEAST likely to be provided by a utility plan is the   18.____

   A. location of the joists and frame members around
   B. stairwells
   C. location of the hot water supply and return piping
   D. location of light fixtures D. number of openings in the floor for radiators

19. According to the passage, the persons who will *most likely* have the GREATEST need for the information included in a utility plan of a building are those who   19.____

   A. maintain and repair the heating system
   B. clean the premises
   C. paint housing exteriors
   D. advertise property for sale

20. According to the passage, a repair crew member should find it MOST helpful to consult a utility plan when information is needed about the   20.____

   A. thickness of all doors in the structure
   B. number of electrical outlets located throughout the structure
   C. dimensions of each window in the structure
   D. length of a roof rafter

KEY (CORRECT ANSWERS)

1. A
2. C
3. B
4. D
5. B

6. A
7. C
8. D
9. D
10. C

11. C
12. A
13. C
14. D
15. B

16. C
17. B
18. A
19. A
20. B

TEST 2

DIRECTIONS: Each question or incomplete statement is followed by several suggested answers or completions. Select the one that BEST answers the question or completes the statement. *PRINT THE LETTER OF THE CORRECT ANSWER IN THE SPACE AT THE RIGHT.*

1. Repair crew men should report accidents on the job IMMEDIATELY *primarily* so that   1._____
   A. the proper person will be reprimanded for his carelessness
   B. a correct count can be kept of time lost through accidents on the job
   C. prompt medical care may be given when needed
   D. the correct forms will be filled out

2. In a circulating hot-water heating system, most boilers have an altitude gauge that shows   2._____
the level of the water in the system. This gauge has two needles, one red, which is set at the proper water level, and one black, which shows the true water level, and which varies with the water-level change. When the red needle is over the black on the gauge, so that they coincide, it means that the system
   A. has too much water
   B. requires more water
   C. is properly filled with water
   D. should be shut off

3. If a radiator fails to heat properly, the FIRST of the following actions which you should   3._____
take is to check the
   A. boiler's steam gauge   B. boiler's water line
   C. radiator's shut-off valve   D. pressure reducing valve

4. Assume that you have been asked to remove a door knob. You inspect the door and find   4._____
that it has a mortise lock, and that the door knob is fastened with a set screw.
Which of the following is the FIRST step that you should take in removing the door knob?
   A. Unscrew the set screw on the slimmest part of the knob
   B. Saw off the knob at its thinnest point
   C. Turn the knob repeatedly to the right and to the left until it finally falls off
   D. Use a pinchbar to spring the lock

5. When preparing a 1:1:6 mix for mortar, how many pails of lime should be added to 3   5._____
pails of sand and 1/2 pail of cement?
   A. 3   B. 1   C. 1/2   D. 1/4

6. If you find that the putty in the can is a little too hard to use, you should add some   6._____
   A. whiting   B. linseed oil
   C. spackle   D. glazing compound

7. The purpose of scratching the surface of the first coat of patching stucco is to 7.____

   A. spread the patching stucco over a wide area
   B. give the surface a textured finish
   C. provide a gripping surface for the next coat of patching stucco
   D. press the patching stucco into the hole to be repaired

8. When filling in large cracks and holes up to 2 inches in diameter in plaster walls it is BEST to use 8.____

   A. spackle   B. patching plaster
   C. gypsum wallboard   D. tile

9. Of the following, the MAIN reason for having a vertical distance of about 7 inches between stair treads is that this 9.____

   A. makes for the best appearance
   B. makes an easy step for the average person
   C. allows for the most profitable use of wood
   D. cuts out a good deal of unnecessary work

10. When removing a door from its hinges to make repairs, it is ALWAYS best to 10.____

    A. remove the pin from the top hinge first
    B. keep the door tightly closed
    C. remove the pin from the bottom hinge first
    D. remove the door knob and lock

11. Dry plaster will absorb water from the patching material, weakening and shrinking it. Based on the information in this statement, it would be *advisable* to take which one of the following actions in the process of patching a plaster crack? 11.____

    A. Mix the plaster with a lot of extra water
    B. Apply water-eased paint to the wall immediately
    C. Apply plaster powder to the crack, then pour water in over it
    D. Dampen the area surrounding the patch with a sponge

12. Standard electrical tools which are safe for ordinary use may be unsafe in locations which contain flammable materials because 12.____

    A. there may be insufficient ventilation
    B. sparks from the tools may start a fire
    C. electric current will usually cause fire
    D. the automatic sprinkler system may be set off accidentally

13. Of the following, the BEST combination of ingredients to use for good concrete is 13.____

    A. cement and water
    B. aggregate and water
    C. cement, sand, stone, and water
    D. gravel, cement, and water

14. If the blade of a screw driver is thicker than the slot at the top of a screw, the way to *properly* drive the screw into wood in this case is to 14.____

    A. widen the slot of the screw to fit the larger blade tip
    B. tap the end of the screw driver lightly to get a firmer hold into the screw slot
    C. get another screw driver which fits the size of the screw slot
    D. apply a drop of lubricating oil to the screw slot to get the screw started into the wood

QUESTIONS 15-20.
Questions 15 through 20 are to be answered *solely* on the basis of the following passage.

The basic hand-operated hoisting device is the tackle or purchase, consisting of a line called a fall, reeved through one or more blocks.

To hoist a load of given size, you must set up a rig with a safe working load equal to or in excess of the load to be hoisted. In order to do this, you must be able to calculate the safe working load of a single part of line of given size; the safe working load of a given purchase which contains a line of given size; and the minimum size of hooks or shackles which you must use in a given type of purchase to hoist a given load. You must also be able to calculate the thrust which a given load will exert on a gin pole or a set of shears inclined at a given angle; the safe working load which a spar of a given size, used as a gin pole or as one of a set of shears, will sustain; and the stress which a given load will set up in the back guy of a gin pole, or in the back guy of a set of shears, inclined at a given angle.

15. The above passage refers to the lifting of loads by means of 15.____

    A. erected scaffolds   B. manual rigging devices
    C. power-driven equipment   D. conveyor belts

16. It can be concluded from the above passage, that a set of shears serves to 16.____

    A. absorb the force and stress of the working load
    B. operate the tackle
    C. contain the working load
    D. compute the safe working load

17. According to the above passage, a spar can be used for a 17.____

    A. back guy   B. block   C. fall   D. gin pole

18. According to the above passage, the rule that a user of hand-operated tackle MUST follow is to make sure that the safe working load is at LEAST 18.____

    A. equal to the weight of the given load
    B. twice the combined weight of the block and falls
    C. one-half the weight of the given load
    D. twice the weight of the given load

19. According to the above passage, the two parts that make up a tackle are 19.____

    A. back guys and gin poles   B. blocksm and falls
    C. rigs and shears   D. spars and shackles

20. According to the above passage, in order to determine whether it is safe to hoist a particular load, you MUST 20._____

    A. use the maximum size hooks
    B. time the speed to bring a given load to a desired place
    C. calculate the forces exerted on various types of rigs
    D. repeatedly lift and lower various loads

KEY (CORRECT ANSWERS)

1.	C	11.	D
2.	C	12.	B
3.	C	13.	C
4.	A	14.	C
5.	C	15.	B
6.	B	16.	A
7.	C	17.	D
8.	B	18.	A
9.	B	19.	B
10.	C	20.	C

EXAMINATION SECTION
TEST 1

DIRECTIONS: Each question or incomplete statement is followed by several suggested answers or completions. Select the one that BEST answers the question or completes the statement. *PRINT THE LETTER OF THE CORRECT ANSWER IN THE SPACE AT THE RIGHT.*

1. Linseed oil putty would MOST likely be used to secure glass in _____ windows.   1.____
    A. steel casement
    B. aluminum jalousie
    C. wood double hung
    D. aluminum storm

2. Of the following, the one type of glass that should NOT be cut with the ordinary type glass cutter is _____ glass.   2.____
    A. safety   B. plate   C. wire   D. herculite

3. Thermopane is made of two sheets of glass separated by   3.____
    A. a sheet of celluloid
    B. wire mesh
    C. an air space
    D. mica

4. Glass is NEVER cut so that it fits snugly inside the frame of a steel casement window. Of the following, the MAIN reason for allowing this space between the glass and the side of the frame is to   4.____
    A. prevent cracking of the glass in cold weather
    B. permit the glass to be lined up properly
    C. allow space for the putty
    D. eliminate the necessity of polishing the edges of the glass

5. Glass is held in steel sash by means of   5.____
    A. points   B. clips   C. plates   D. blocks

6. When nailing felt to a roof, the nails should be driven through a   6.____
    A. tinned disc
    B. steel washer
    C. brass plate
    D. plastic bushing

7. An opening in a parapet wall for draining water from a roof is MOST often called a   7.____
    A. leader   B. gutter   C. downspout   D. scupper

8. Roofing nails are usually   8.____
    A. brass
    B. cement coated
    C. galvanized
    D. nickel plated

9. A *street ell* is a fitting having   9.____
    A. male threads at both ends
    B. male threads at one end and female threads at the other end
    C. female threads at both ends
    D. male threads at one end and a solder connection at the other end

23

10. Of the following pieces of equipment, the one on which you would MOST likely find a safety (pop-off) valve is a(n)

    A. hot air furnace
    B. air conditioning compressor
    C. hot water heater
    D. dehumidifier

11. Compression fittings are MOST often used with

    A. cast iron bell and spigot pipe
    B. steel flange pipe
    C. copper tubing
    D. transite

12. Water hammer is BEST eliminated by

    A. increasing the size of all the piping
    B. installing an air chamber
    C. replacing the valve seats with neoprene gaskets
    D. flushing the system to remove corrosion

13. The BEST type of pipe to use in a gas line in a domestic installation is

    A. black iron
    B. galvanized iron
    C. cast iron
    D. wrought steel

14. If there is a pinhole in the float of a toilet tank, the

    A. water will flush continually
    B. toilet cannot flush
    C. tank cannot be filled with water
    D. valve will not shut off so water will overflow into the overflow tube

15. Condensation of moisture in humid weather occurs MOST often on _____ pipe(s).

    A. sewage
    B. gas
    C. hot water
    D. cold water

16. A gas appliance should be connected to a gas line by means of a(n)

    A. union
    B. right and left coupling
    C. elbow
    D. close nipple

17. A PRINCIPAL difference between a pipe thread and a machine thread is that the pipe thread is

    A. tapered   B. finer   C. flat   D. longer

18. When joining galvanized iron pipe, pipe joint compound is placed on

    A. the female threads only
    B. the male threads only
    C. both the male and female threads
    D. either the male or the female threads depending on the type of fitting

19. If moisture is trapped between the layers of a 3-ply roof, the heat of a summer day will   19.____

    A. dry the roof out
    B. cause blisters to be formed in the roofing
    C. rot the felt material
    D. have no effect on the roofing

20. Of the following, the metal MOST often used for leaders and gutters is   20.____

    A. monel   B. brass
    C. steel   D. galvanized iron

21. When drilling a small hole in sheet copper, the BEST practice is to   21.____

    A. make a dent with a center punch first
    B. put some cutting oil at the point you intend to drill
    C. use a slow speed drill to prevent overheating
    D. use an auger type bit

22. The reason for annealing sheet copper is to make it   22.____

    A. soft and easier to work
    B. more resistant to weather
    C. easier to solder
    D. harder and more resistant to blows

23. In draw filing,   23.____

    A. only the edge of the file is used
    B. a triangle file is generally used
    C. the file is pulled toward the mechanic's body in filing
    D. the file must have a safe edge

24. The type of paint that uses water as a thinner is   24.____

    A. enamel   B. latex   C. shellac   D. lacquer

25. The reason for placing a 6" sub-base of cinders under a concrete sidewalk is to   25.____

    A. provide flexibility in the surface
    B. permit drainage of water
    C. prevent chemicals in the soil from damaging the sidewalk
    D. allow room for the concrete to expand

26. The BEST material to use to lubricate a door lock is   26.____

    A. penetrating oil   B. pike oil
    C. graphite   D. light grease

27. Assume that the color of the flame from a gas stove is bright yellow. To correct this, you should   27.____

    A. close the air flap
    B. open the air flap
    C. increase the gas pressure
    D. increase the size of the gas opening

28. In a 110-220 volt three-wire circuit, the neutral wire is usually

    A. black   B. red   C. white   D. green

29. Brushes on fractional horsepower universal motors are MOST often made of

    A. flexible copper strands
    B. rigid carbon blocks
    C. thin wire strips
    D. collector rings

30. Leaks from the stem of a faucet can generally be stopped by replacing the

    A. bibb washer   B. seat   C. packing   D. gasket

31. Of the following, the BEST procedure to follow with a frozen water pipe is to

    A. allow the pipe to thaw out by itself as the weather gets warmer
    B. put anti-freeze into the pipe above the section that is frozen
    C. turn on the hot water heater
    D. open the faucet closest to the frozen pipe and warm the pipe with a blow torch, starting at this point

32. The one of the following that is NOT usually changed by a central air conditioning system is the

    A. volume of air in the system
    B. humidity of the air
    C. dust in the air
    D. air pressure of the system

33. The temperature of a domestic hot water system is MOST often controlled by a(n)

    A. relief valve   B. aquastat   C. barometer   D. thermostat

34. Draft in a chimney is MOST often controlled by a(n)

    A. damper
    B. gate
    C. orifice
    D. cross connection

35. Assume that a refrigerator motor operates continuously for excessively long periods of time.
    The FIRST item you should check to locate the defect is the

    A. plug in the outlet
    B. door gasket
    C. direction of rotation of the motor
    D. motor switch

36. Assume that after replacing a defective motor for a large electric fan, you find that the fan is rotating in the wrong direction.
    If the motor is a split phase motor, with the shaft at one end only, the trouble could be CORRECTED by

    A. reversing the fan on its shaft
    B. turning the motor end for end
    C. interchanging the connections on the field terminals of the motor
    D. reversing the plug in the electric outlet

37. In order to properly hang a door, shims are frequently inserted under the hinges. These shims are MOST often made of

   A. cardboard
   B. sheet steel
   C. bakelite
   D. the same materials as the hinges

38. Flooring nails are usually _____ nails.

   A. casing   B. common   C. cut   D. clinch

39. Over a doorway, to support brick, you will usually find

   A. steel angles   B. hanger bolts
   C. wooden headers   D. stirrups

40. Insulation of steam pipes is MOST often done with

   A. asbestos   B. celotex   C. alundum   D. sheathing

41. Assume that only the first few coils of a hot water convector used for heating a room are hot.
    To correct this, you should FIRST

   A. increase the water pressure
   B. increase the water temperature
   C. bleed the air out of the convector
   D. clean the convector pipes

42. The MAIN reason for grounding the outer sheel of an electric fixture is to

   A. provide additional support for the fixture
   B. reduce the cost of installation of the fixture
   C. provide a terminal to which the wires can be attached
   D. reduce the chance of electric shock

43. In woodwork, countersinking is MOST often done for

   A. lag screws   B. carriage bolts
   C. hanger bolts   D. flat head screws

44. Bridging is MOST often used in connection with

   A. door frames   B. window openings
   C. floor joists   D. stud walls

45. A saddle is part of a

   A. doorway   B. window
   C. stair well   D. bulkhead

46. To make it easier to drive screws into hard wood, it is BEST to 46.____
    A. use a screwdriver that is longer than that used for soft wood
    B. rub the threads of the screw on a bar of soap
    C. oil the screw threads
    D. use a square shank screwdriver assisted by a wrench

47. In using a doweled joint to make a repair of a wooden door, it is important to remember 47.____
    that the dowel
    A. hole must be smaller in diameter than the dowel so that there is a tight fit
    B. hole must be longer than the dowel to provide a room for excess glue
    C. must be of the same type of wood as the door frame
    D. must be held in place by a small screw while waiting for the glue to set

48. The edges of MOST finished wood flooring are 48.____
    A. tongue and groove   B. mortise and tenon
    C. bevel and miter   D. lap and scarf

49. For the SMOOTHEST finish, sanding of wood should be done 49.____
    A. in a circular direction
    B. diagonally against the grain
    C. across the grain
    D. parallel with the grain

50. To prevent splintering of wood when boring a hole through it, the BEST practice is to 50.____
    A. drill at a slow speed
    B. use a scrap piece to back up the work
    C. use an auger bit
    D. ease up the pressure on the drill when the drill is almost through the wood

KEY (CORRECT ANSWERS)

1. C	11. C	21. A	31. D	41. C
2. D	12. B	22. A	32. D	42. D
3. C	13. A	23. C	33. B	43. D
4. A	14. D	24. B	34. A	44. C
5. B	15. D	25. B	35. B	45. A
6. A	16. B	26. C	36. C	46. B
7. D	17. A	27. B	37. A	47. B
8. C	18. B	28. C	38. C	48. A
9. B	19. B	29. B	39. A	49. D
10. C	20. D	30. C	40. A	50. B

TEST 2

DIRECTIONS: Each question or incomplete statement is followed by several suggested answers or completions. Select the one that BEST answers the question or completes the statement. *PRINT THE LETTER OF THE CORRECT ANSWER IN THE SPACE AT THE RIGHT.*

1. A *speed nut* has

    A. no threads
    B. threads that are coarser than a standard nut
    C. threads that are finer than s standard nut
    D. fewer threads than a standard nut

    1.____

2. The BEST tool to use to remove the burr and sharp edge resulting from cutting tubing with a tube cutter is a

    A. file B. scraper C. reamer D. knife

    2.____

3. A router is used PRINCIPALLY to

    A. clean pipe
    B. cut grooves in wood
    C. bend electric conduit
    D. sharpen tools

    3.____

4. The principle of operation of a sabre saw is MOST similar to that of a _____ saw.

    A. circular B. radial C. swing D. jig

    4.____

5. A full thread cutting set would have both taps and

    A. cutters B. bushings C. dies D. plugs

    5.____

6. The proper flux to use for soldering electric wire connections is

    A. rosin
    B. killed acid
    C. borax
    D. zinc chloride

    6.____

7. A fusestat differs from an ordinary plug fuse in that a fusestat has

    A. less current carrying capacity
    B. different size threads
    C. an aluminum shell instead of a copper shell
    D. no threads

    7.____

8. A grounding type 120-volt receptacle differs from an ordinary electric receptacle MAINLY in that a grounding receptacle

    A. is larger than the ordinary receptacle
    B. has openings for a three prong plug
    C. can be used for larger machinery
    D. has a built-in circuit breaker

    8.____

9. A carbide tip is MOST often found on a bit used for drilling

    A. concrete B. wood C. steel D. brass

    9.____

10. The MAIN reason for using oil on an oilstone is to

   A. make the surface of the stone smoother
   B. prevent clogging of the pores of the stone
   C. reduce the number of times the stone has to be *dressed*
   D. prevent gouging of the stone's surface

11. The sum of the following numbers, 1 3/4, 3 1/6, 5 1/2, 6 5/8, and 9 1/4, is

   A. 26 1/8   B. 26 1/4   C. 26 1/2   D. 26 3/4

12. If a piece of plywood measures 5' 1 1/4" x 3' 2 1/2", the number of square feet in this board is MOST NEARLY

   A. 15.8   B. 16.1   C. 16.4   D. 16.7

13. Assume that in quantity purchases the city receives a discount of 33 1/3%.
   If a one gallon can of paint retails at $5.33 per gallon, the cost of 375 gallons of this paint is MOST NEARLY

   A. $1,332.50   B. $1,332.75   C. $1,333.00   D. $1,333.25

14. Assume that eight barrels of cement together weigh a total of 3004 lbs. and 12 oz.
   If there are four bags of cement per barrel, then the weight of one bag of cement is MOST NEARLY _____ lbs.

   A. 93.1   B. 93.5   C. 93.9   D. 94.3

15. Assume that one man cuts 50 nameplates per hour, whereas his co-worker cuts 55 nameplates per hour.
   At the end of 7 hours, the first man will have cut fewer nameplates than the second man by

   A. 9.3%   B. 9.5%   C. 9.7%   D. 9.9%

16. Under the same conditions, the one of the following that dries the FASTEST is

   A. shellac   B. varnish   C. enamel   D. lacquer

17. Interior wood trim in a building is MOST often made of

   A. hemlock   B. pine   C. cedar   D. oak

18. Gaskets are seldom made of

   A. rubber   B. lead   C. asbestos   D. vinyl

19. Toggle bolts are MOST frequently used to

   A. fasten shelf supports to a hollow block wall
   B. fasten furniture legs to table tops
   C. anchor machinery to a concrete floor
   D. join two pieces of sheet metal

20. Rubber will deteriorate FASTEST when it is constantly in contact with

   A. air   B. water   C. oil   D. soapsuds

21. Stoppage of water flow is often caused by dirt accumulating in an elbow. 21.____
    As used in the above sentence, the word accumulating means MOST NEARLY

    A. clogging   B. collecting   C. rusting   D. confined

22. The surface of the metal was embossed. 22.____
    As used in the above sentence, the word embossed means MOST NEARLY

    A. polished   B. rough   C. raised   D. painted

Questions 23-24.

DIRECTIONS: Questions 23 and 24 are to be answered in accordance with the following paragraph.

When fixing an upper sash cord, you must also remove the lower sash. To do this, the parting strip between the sash must be removed. Now remove the cover from the weight box channel, cut off the cord as before, and pull it over the pulleys. Pull your new cord over the pulleys and down into the channel, where it may be fastened to the weight. The cord for an upper sash is cut off 1" or 2" below the pulley with the weight resting on the floor of the pocket and the cord held taut. These measurements allow for slight stretching of the cord. When the cord is cut to length, it can be pulled up over the pulley and tied with a single common knot in the end to fit into the socket in the sash groove. If the knot protrudes beyond the face of the sash, tap it gently to flatten. In this way, it will not become frayed from constant rubbing against the groove.

23. When repairing the upper sash cord, the FIRST thing to do is to 23.____

    A. remove the lower sash
    B. cut the existing sash cord
    C. remove the parting strip
    D. measure the length of new cord necessary

24. According to the above paragraph, the rope may become frayed if the 24.____

    A. pulley is too small   B. knot sticks out
    C. cord is too long   D. weight is too heavy

25. In the repair of the sash cord mentioned in the paragraph for Questions 23 and 24, the 25.____
    MAIN reason for cutting off the sash cord below the bottom of the pulley is to

    A. prevent the cord from tangling
    B. save on amount of cord used
    C. prevent the sash weight from hitting the bottom of the frame in use
    D. provide room for tying the knot

26. Of the following drawings, the one that would be considered an *elevation* of a building is 26.____
    the

    A. floor plan   B. front view   C. cross section   D. site plan

27. On a plan, the symbol shown at the right USUALLY represents a(n) 27.____

    A. duplex receptacle   B. electric switch
    C. ceiling outlet   D. pull box

28. On a plan, the symbol _____ - _____ - USUALLY represents a

    A. center line
    B. hidden outline
    C. long break
    D. dimension line

29. Assume that on a plan you see the following: 1/4" - 20 NC-2. This refers to the

    A. diameter of a hole
    B. size and type of screw thread
    C. taper of a pin
    D. scale at which the plan is drawn

30. In reference to the above sketch, the length of the diagonal part of the plate indicated by the question mark is MOST NEARLY

    A. 13"   B. 14"   C. 15"   D. 16"

31. To increase the workability of concrete without changing its strength, the BEST procedure to follow is to increase the percentage of

    A. water
    B. cement and sand
    C. cement and water
    D. water and sand

32. The MAIN reason for covering freshly poured concrete with tar paper is to

    A. prevent evaporation of water
    B. stop people from walking on the concrete
    C. protect the concrete from rain
    D. keep back any earth that may fall on the concrete

33. The MAIN reason for using air-entrained cement in sidewalks is to

    A. protect the concrete from the effects of freezing
    B. color the concrete
    C. speed up the setting time of the concrete
    D. make the concrete more workable

34. Assume that a reinforcing bar used for concrete is badly rusted. Before using this bar,

    A. it is not necessary to remove any rust
    B. only loose rust need be removed
    C. all rust should be removed
    D. all rust should be removed and a coat of red lead paint is applied

35. Assume that freshly poured concrete has been exposed to freezing temperatures for 6 hours.
    In all likelihood, this concrete

    A. has been permanently damaged
    B. will harden properly as soon as the air temperature warms up
    C. will harden properly even though the temperature remains below freezing
    D. will eventually harden properly, but it will take much longer than usual

36. Assume that concrete for a floor in a play yard is to be placed directly on the earth. On checking, you find that, because of a recent rain, the earth is damp.
    You should

    A. wait till the sun dries the earth before placing the concrete
    B. use a waterproofing material between the concrete slab and the earth
    C. use less water in the concrete mix
    D. ignore the damp earth and place the concrete as you normally would

37. The MAJOR disadvantage of *floating* the surface of concrete too much is that the

    A. surface will become too rough
    B. surface will become weak and will wear rapidly
    C. initial set will be disturbed
    D. concrete cannot be cured properly

38. In addition to water and sand, mortar mix for a cinder block wall is usually made of

    A. gravel and lime
    B. plaster and cement
    C. gravel and cement
    D. lime and cement

39. The *nominal* size of a standard cinder block is

    A. 8" x 6" x 16"
    B. 8" x 8" x 16"
    C. 8" x 12" x 12"
    D. 6" x 8" x 12"

40. The *bond* of a brick wall refers to the

    A. arrangement of headers and stretchers
    B. time it takes for the mortar to set
    C. way a brick wall is tied in to an intersecting wall
    D. type of mortar used in the wall

41. The purpose of *tooling* when erecting a brick wall is to

    A. cut the brick to fit into a small space
    B. insure that the brick is laid level
    C. compact the mortar at the joints
    D. hold the brick in place till the mortar sets

42. Mortar is BEST cleaned off the face of a brick wall by using 42.____

    A. muriatic acid B. lye
    C. oxalic acid D. sodium hypochlorite

43. A brick wall is *pointed* to 43.____

    A. make sure it is the correct height
    B. repair the mortar joints
    C. set the brick in place
    D. arrange the mortar bed before setting the brick

44. The second coat in a three-coat plaster job is the _____ coat. 44.____

    A. scratch B. brown C. putty D. lime

45. To repair fine cracks in a plastered wall, the PROPER material to use is 45.____

    A. lime B. cement wash
    C. perlite D. spackle

46. Gypsum lath for plastering is purchased in 46.____

    A. strips 5/16" x 1 1/2" x 4'
    B. rolls 3/8" x 48" x 96"
    C. boards 1/2" x 16" x 48"
    D. sheets 5/16" x 27" x 96"

47. The PRINCIPAL reason for using acoustic tile instead of ordinary tile is that the acoustic tile 47.____

    A. deadens sound B. is easier to apply
    C. is longer lasting D. costs less

48. The MAXIMUM thickness of the finish coat of white plaster is MOST NEARLY 48.____

    A. 1/8" B. 1/4" C. 3/8" D. 1/2"

49. When using tape to conceal joints in dry wall construction, the FIRST operation is 49.____

    A. channelling the grooves between boards
    B. applying cement to the joints
    C. sanding the edges of the joints
    D. packing the tape into the joints

50. For the FIRST coat of plaster on wire lath, plaster of paris is mixed with 50.____

    A. cement B. sand C. lime D. mortar

KEY (CORRECT ANSWERS)

1. A	11. B	21. B	31. C	41. C
2. C	12. C	22. C	32. A	42. A
3. B	13. A	23. C	33. A	43. B
4. D	14. C	24. B	34. B	44. B
5. C	15. D	25. C	35. A	45. D
6. A	16. D	26. B	36. D	46. C
7. B	17. B	27. C	37. B	47. A
8. B	18. D	28. A	38. D	48. A
9. A	19. A	29. B	39. B	49. B
10. B	20. C	30. A	40. A	50. B

EXAMINATION SECTION
TEST 1

DIRECTIONS: Each question or incomplete statement is followed by several suggested answers or completions. Select the one that BEST answers the question or completes the statement. *PRINT THE LETTER OF THE CORRECT ANSWER IN THE SPACE AT THE RIGHT.*

1.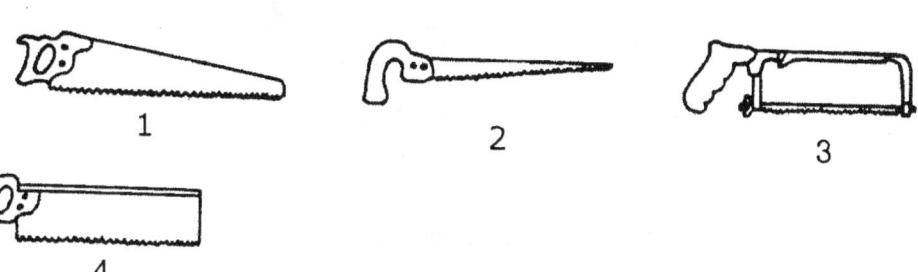

   The saw that is used PRINCIPALLY where curved cuts are to be made is numbered

   A. 1   B. 2   C. 3   D. 4

   1.____

2.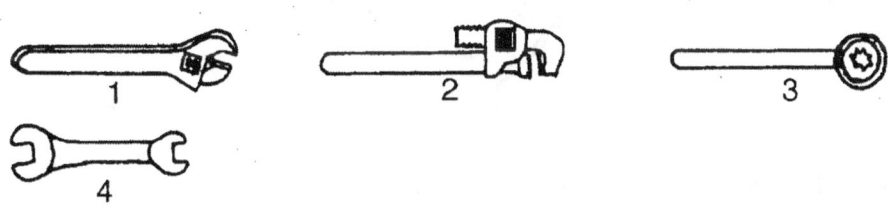

   The wrench that is used PRINCIPALLY for pipe work is numbered

   A. 1   B. 2   C. 3   D. 4

   2.____

3.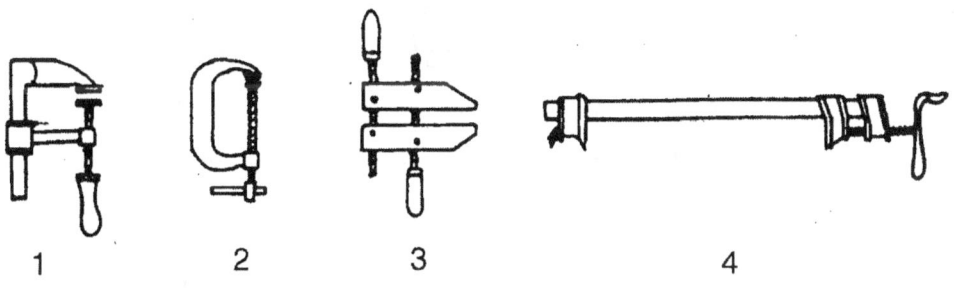

   The carpenter's *hand screw* is numbered

   A. 1   B. 2   C. 3   D. 4

   3.____

4.

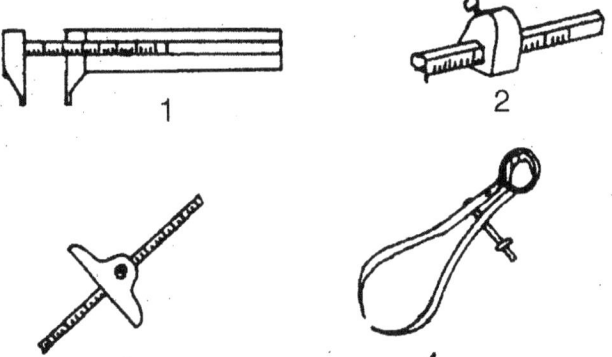

The tool used to measure the depth of a hole is numbered

A. 1   B. 2   C. 3   D. 4

5.

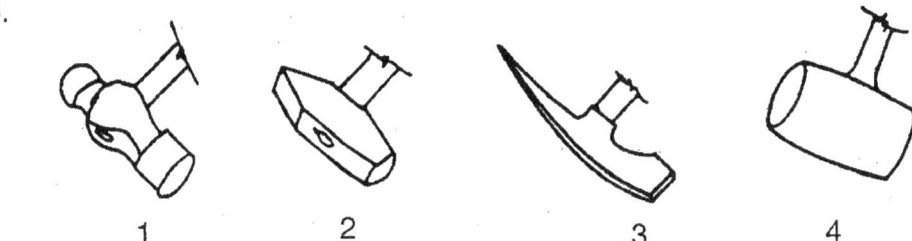

The tool that is BEST suited for use with a wood chisel is numbered

A. 1   B. 2   C. 3   D. 4

6.

The screw head that would be tightened with an *Allen* wrench is numbered

A. 1   B. 2   C. 3   D. 4

7.

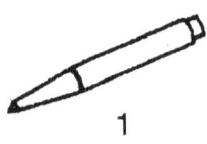 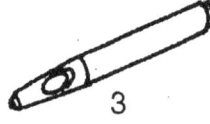

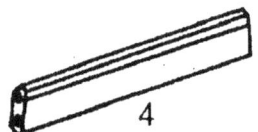

The center punch is numbered

A. 1   B. 2   C. 3   D. 4

8.

The tool used to drill a hole in concrete is numbered

A. 1   B. 2   C. 3   D. 4

9.

The wrench whose PRINCIPAL purpose to to hold taps for threading is numbered

A. 1   B. 2   C. 3   D. 4

10.

The electrician's bit is indicated by the number

A. 1   B. 2   C. 3   D. 4

11. The ends of a joist in a brick building are cut to a bevel. This is done PRINCIPALLY to prevent damage to

A. joist   B. floor   C. sill   D. wall

12. Of the following, the wood that is MOST commonly used today for floor joists is   12._____

    A. long leaf yellow pine   B. douglas fir
    C. oak   D. birch

13. Quarter-sawed lumber is preferred for the BEST finished flooring PRINCIPALLY because   13._____
    it

    A. has the greatest strength   B. shrinks the least
    C. is the easiest to nail   D. is the easiest to handle

14. A tool used in hanging doors is a   14._____

    A. miter gauge   B. line level
    C. try square   D. butt gauge

15. Of the following, the MAXIMUM height that would be considered acceptable for a stair   15._____
    riser is

    A. 6 1/2"   B. 7 1/2"   C. 8 1/2"   D. 9 1/2"

16. The PRINCIPAL reason for *cross banding* the layers of wood in a plywood panel is to   16._____
    _____ of the panel.

    A. reduce warping   B. increase the strength
    C. reduce the cost   D. increase the beauty

17. The part of a tree that will produce the DENSEST wood is the _____ wood.   17._____

    A. spring   B. summer   C. sap   D. heart

18. Casing nails MOST NEARLY resemble _____ nails.   18._____

    A. common   B. roofing   C. form   D. finishing

19. Lumber in quantity is ordered by   19._____

    A. cubic feet   B. foot board measure
    C. lineal feet   D. weight and length

20. For finishing of wood, BEST results are obtained by sanding   20._____

    A. with a circular motion
    B. against the grain
    C. with the grain
    D. with a circular motion on edges and against the grain on the flat parts

21. A *chase* in a brick wall is a   21._____

    A. pilaster   B. waterstop   C. recess   D. corbel

22. Parging refers to   22._____

    A. increasing the thickness of a brick wall
    B. plastering the back of face brickwork
    C. bonding face brick to backing blocks
    D. leveling each course of brick

23. The PRINCIPAL reason for requiring brick to be wetted before laying is that

    A. less water is required in the mortar
    B. efflorescence is prevented
    C. the brick will not absorb as much water from the mortar
    D. cool brick is easier to handle

24. In brickwork, muriatic acid is commonly used to

    A. increase the strength of the mortar
    B. etch the brick
    C. waterproof the wall
    D. clean the wall

25. Cement mortar can be made easier to work by the addition of a small quantity of

    A. lime   B. soda   C. litharge   D. plaster

26. Headers in brickwork are used to _____ the wall.

    A. strengthen   B. reduce the cost of
    C. speed the erection of   D. align

27. Joints in brick walls are tooled

    A. immediately after each brick is laid
    B. after the mortar has had its initial set
    C. after the entire wall is completed
    D. 28 days after the wall has been built

28. If cement mortar has begun to set before it can be used in a wall, the BEST thing to do is to

    A. use the mortar immediately as is
    B. add a small quantity of lime
    C. add some water and mix thoroughly
    D. discard the mortar

29. A *bat* in brickwork is a

    A. brace to hold a wall temporarily in place
    B. stick used to aid in mixing of mortar
    C. broken piece of brick used to fill short spaces
    D. curved brick used in ornamental work

30. The proportions by volume of cement, lime, and sand in a cement-lime mortar should be, according to the Building Code,

    A. 1:1:3   B. 2:1:6   C. 1:1:6   D. 1:2:6

31. The BEST flux to use when soldering galvanized iron is

    A. killed acid   B. sal-ammoniac
    C. muriatic acid   D. resin

32. When soldering a vertical joint, the soldering iron should be tinned on _____ side(s). 32.____
    A. 1 B. 2 C. 3 D. 4

33. The difference between *right hand* and *left hand* tin snips is the 33.____
    A. relative position of the cutting jaws
    B. shape of the cutting jaws
    C. shape of the handles
    D. relative position of the handles

34. A machine used to bend sheet metal is called a 34.____
    A. router B. planer C. brake D. swage

35. The type of solder that would be used in *hard soldering* would be _____ solder. 35.____
    A. bismuth B. wiping C. 50-50 D. silver

36. Roll roofing material is usually felt which has been impregnated with 36.____
    A. cement B. mastic C. tar D. latex

37. The purpose of flashing on roofs is to 37.____
    A. secure roofing materials to the roof
    B. make it easier to lay the roofing
    C. prevent leaks through the roof
    D. insulate the roof from excessive heat

38. The tool used to spread hot pitch on a three-ply roofing job is a 38.____
    A. mop B. spreader C. pusher D. broom

39. The cutting of glass can be facilitated by dipping the cutting wheel in 39.____
    A. *3-in-1* oil B. water C. lard D. kerosene

40. The strips of metal used to hold glass to the window frame while it is being puttied are called 40.____
    A. hold-downs B. points C. wedges D. triangles

41. The type of chain used with sash weights is _____ link. 41.____
    A. flat   B. round
    C. figure-eight   D. basket-weave

42. The material that would be used to seal around a window frame is 42.____
    A. oakum B. litharge C. grout D. calking

43. The function of a window sill is MOST NEARLY the same as that of a 43.____
    A. jamb B. coping C. lintel D. brick

44. Lightweight plaster would be made with 44.____
    A. sand B. cinders C. potash D. vermiculite

45. The FIRST coat of plaster to be applied on a three-coat plaster job is the _____ coat. 45.____
    A. brown   B. scratch   C. white   D. keene

46. Screeds in plaster work are used to 46.____
    A. remove larger sizes of sand
    B. hold the batch of plaster before it is applied
    C. apply the plaster to the wall
    D. guide the plasterer in making, an even wall

47. The FIRST coat of plaster over rock lath should be a _____ plaster. 47.____
    A. gypsum   B. lime
    C. portland cement   D. puzzolan cement

48. In plastering, a *hawk* is used to _____ plaster. 48.____
    A. apply   B. hold   C. scratch   D. smooth

49. When mixing concrete by hand, the order in which the ingredients should be mixed is: 49.____
    A. water, cement, sand, stone
    B. sand, cement, water, stone
    C. stone, water, sand, cement
    D. stone, sand, cement, water

50. The PRINCIPAL reason for covering a concrete sidewalk with straw or paper after the concrete has been poured is to 50.____
    A. prevent people from walking on the concrete while it is still wet
    B. impart a rough non-slip surface to the concrete
    C. prevent excessive evaporation of water in the concrete
    D. shorten the length of time it would take for the concrete to harden

KEY (CORRECT ANSWERS)

1. B	11. D	21. C	31. C	41. A
2. B	12. B	22. B	32. A	42. D
3. C	13. B	23. C	33. A	43. B
4. C	14. D	24. D	34. C	44. D
5. D	15. B	25. A	35. D	45. B
6. C	16. A	26. A	36. C	46. D
7. A	17. D	27. B	37. C	47. A
8. D	18. D	28. D	38. A	48. B
9. A	19. B	29. C	39. D	49. D
10. C	20. C	30. C	40. B	50. C

TEST 2

DIRECTIONS: Each question or incomplete statement is followed by several suggested answers or completions. Select the one that BEST answers the question or completes the statement. *PRINT THE LETTER OF THE CORRECT ANSWER IN THE SPACE AT THE RIGHT.*

1. When colored concrete is required, the colors used should be   1.____
    - A. colors in oil
    - B. mineral pigments
    - C. tempera colors
    - D. water colors

2. Concrete is *rubbed* with a(n)   2.____
    - A. emery wheel
    - B. carborundum brick
    - C. sandstone
    - D. alundum stick

3. To prevent concrete from sticking to forms, the forms should be painted with   3.____
    - A. oil
    - B. kerosene
    - C. water
    - D. lime

4. The reinforcement in a concrete floor slab is referred to as 6"-6" x #6-#6. The type of reinforcing that is being used is   4.____
    - A. steel bars
    - B. wire mesh
    - C. angle irons
    - D. grating plate

5. One method of measuring the consistency of a concrete mix is by means of a _____ test.   5.____
    - A. penetration
    - B. flow
    - C. slump
    - D. weight

6. A chemical that is sometimes used to prevent the freezing of concrete in cold weather is   6.____
    - A. alum
    - B. glycerine
    - C. calcium chloride
    - D. sodium nitrate

7. The one of the following that is LEAST commonly used for columns is   7.____
    - A. wide flange beams
    - B. angles
    - C. concrete-filled pipe
    - D. I beams

8. Fire protection of steel floor beams is MOST frequently accomplished by the use of   8.____
    - A. gypsum block
    - B. brick
    - C. rock wool fill
    - D. vermiculite gypsum plaster

9. A *Pittsburgh lock* is a(n)   9.____
    - A. emergency door lock
    - B. sheet metal joint
    - C. elevator safety
    - D. boiler valve

10. In order to drill a hole at right angle to the horizontal axis of a round bar, the bar should be held in a   10.____
    - A. step block
    - B. C-block
    - C. hand pliers
    - D. V-block

11. The procedure to follow in the lubrication of maintenance shop equipment is to lubricate

    A. when you can spare the time
    B. only when necessary
    C. at regular intervals
    D. when the equipment is in operation

12. Of the following items, the one which is NOT used in making fastenings to masonry or plaster walls is a(n)

    A. lead shield   B. expansion bolt
    C. rawl plug   D. steel bushing

13. When a common straight ladder is used to paint a wall, the safe distance that the foot of the ladder should be set away from the wall is MOST NEARLY _____ the length of the ladder.

    A. one-eighth   B. one-quarter
    C. one-half   D. five-eighths

14. The term *bell and spigot* usually refers to

    A. refrigerator motors   B. cast iron pipes
    C. steam radiator outlets   D. electrical receptacles

15. In plumbing work, a valve which allows water to flow in one direction only is commonly known as a _____ valve.

    A. check   B. globe   C. gate   D. stop

16. A pipe coupling is BEST used to connect two pieces of pipe of

    A. the same diameter in a straight line
    B. the same diameter at right angles to each other
    C. different diameters at a 45° angle
    D. different diameters at an 1/8th bend

17. A fitting or pipe with many outlets relatively close together is commonly called a

    A. manifold   B. gooseneck
    C. flange union   D. return bend

18. To locate the center in the end of a sound shaft, the BEST tool to use is a(n)

    A. ruler   B. divider
    C. hermaphrodite caliper D. micrometer

19. When cutting a piece of 1 1/4" O.D. 20 gauge brass tubing with a hand hacksaw, it is BEST to use a blade having _____ teeth per inch.

    A. 14   B. 18   C. 22   D. 32

20. When cutting a piece of 1" O.D. extra-heavy pipe with a pipe cutter, a burr usually forms on the inside and the outside of the pipe. These burrs are BEST removed by means of a pipe

    A. tap and a file   B. wrench and rough stone
    C. reamer and a file   D. drill and a chisel

21. Artificial respiration should be started immediately on a man who has suffered an electric shock if he is

    A. *unconscious* and breathing
    B. *unconscious* and not breathing
    C. *conscious* and in a daze
    D. *conscious* and badly burned

22. The fuse of a certain circuit has blown and is replaced with a fuse of the same rating which also blows when the switch is closed.
    In this case,

    A. a fuse of higher current rating should be used
    B. a fuse of higher voltage rating should be used
    C. the fuse should be temporarily replaced by a heavy piece of wire
    D. the circuit should be checked

23. Operating an incandescent electric light bulb at less than its rated voltage will result in

    A. shorter life and brighter light
    B. longer life and dimmer light
    C. brighter light and longer life
    D. dimmer light and shorter life

24. In order to control a lamp from two different positions, it is necessary to use

    A. two single pole switches
    B. one single pole switch and one four-way switch
    C. two three-way switches
    D. one single pole switch and one four-way switch

25. One method of testing fuses is to connect a pair of test lamps in the circuit in such a manner that the test lamp will light up if the fuse is good and will remain dark if the fuse is bad. In the above illustration 1 and 2 are fuses.
    In order to test if fuse 1 is bad, test lamps should be connected between

    A. A and B   B. B and D   C. A and D   D. C and B

26. The PRINCIPAL reason for the grounding of electrical equipment and circuits is to

    A. prevent short circuits   B. insure safety from shock
    C. save power   D. increase voltage

27. The ordinary single-pole flush wall type switch must be connected

    A. across the line
    B. in the *hot* conductor
    C. in the grounded conductor
    D. in the white conductor

28. A D.C. shunt motor runs in the wrong direction. This fault can be CORRECTED by

    A. reversing the connections of both the field and the armature
    B. interchanging the connections of either main or auxiliar windings
    C. interchanging the connections to either the field or the armature windings
    D. interchanging the connections to the line of the power leads

29. The MOST common type of motor that can be used with both A.C. and D.C. sources is the _____ motor.

    A. compound   B. repulsion   C. series   D. shunt

30. A fluorescent fixture in a new building has been in use for several months without trouble. Recently, the ends of the fluorscent lamp have remained lighted when the light was switched off.
    The BEST way to clear up this trouble is to replace the

    A. lamp   B. ballast   C. starter   D. sockets

31. The BEST wood to use for handles of tools such as axes and hammers is

    A. hemlock   B. pine   C. oak   D. hickory

32. A *hanger bolt*

    A. has a square head
    B. is bent in a *U* shape
    C. has a different type of thread at each end
    D. is threaded the entire length from point to head

33. A stone frequently used to sharpen tools is

    A. carborundum   B. bauxite   C. resin   D. slate

34. A strike plate is MOST closely associated with a

    A. lock   B. sash   C. butt   D. tie rod

35. The material that distinguishes a terrazzo floor from an ordinary concrete floor is

    A. cinders
    B. marble chip
    C. cut stone
    D. non-slip aggregate

36. A room is 7'6" wide by 9'0" long with a ceiling height of 8'0". One gallon of flat paint will cover approximately 400 square feet of wall.
    The number of gallons of this paint required to paint the walls of this room, making no deductions for windows or doors, is MOST NEARLY _____ gallon.

    A. 1/4   B. 1/2   C. 3/4   D. 1

37. The cost of a certain job is broken down as follows:
    Materials $375
    Rental of equipment   120
    Labor   315
    The percentage of the total cost of the job that can be charged to materials is MOST NEARLY

    A. 40%   B. 42%   C. 44%   D. 46%

38. By trial, it is found that by using two cubic feet of sand, a five cubic foot batch of concrete is produced.
    Using the same proportions, the amount of sand required to produce 2 cubic yards of concrete is MOST NEARLY _____ cu.ft.

    A. 20   B. 22   C. 24   D. 26

39. It takes 4 men 6 days to do a certain job.
    Working at the same speed, the number of days it will take 3 men to do this job is

    A. 7   B. 8   C. 9   D. 10

40. The cost of rawl plugs is $2.75 per gross. The cost of 2,448 rawl plugs is

    A. $46.75   B. $47.25   C. $47.75   D. $48.25

41. *Rigidity* of the hammer handle enables the operator to control and direct the force of the blow.
    As used above, *rigidity* means MOST NEARLY

    A. straightness   B. strength
    C. shape   D. stiffness

42. *For precision work, center punches are ground to a fine tapered point.* As used above, *tapered* means MOST NEARLY

    A. conical   B. straight   C. accurate   D. smooth

43. *There are limitations to the drilling of metals by hand power.*
    As used above, *limitations* means MOST NEARLY

    A. advantages   B. restrictions
    C. difficulties   D. benefits

Questions 44-45.

DIRECTIONS: Questions 44 and 45 are based on the following paragraph.

Because electric drills run at high speed, the cutting edges of a twist drill are heated quickly. If the metal is thick, the drill point must be withdrawn from the hole frequently to cool it and clear out chips. Forcing the drill continuously into a deep hole will heat it, thereby spoiling its temper and cutting edges. A portable electric drill has the advantage that it can be taken to the work and used to drill holes in material too large to handle in a drill press.

44. According to the above paragraph, overheating of a twist drill will

    A. slow down the work   B. cause excessive drill breakage
    C. dull the drill   D. spoil the accuracy of the work

45. According to the above paragraph, one method of preventing overheating of a twist drill is to 45.____

   A. use cooling oil
   B. drill a smaller pilot hole first
   C. use a drill press
   D. remove the drill from the work frequently

Questions 46-50.

DIRECTIONS: Questions 46 to 50 are to be answered in accordance with the sketch shown below.

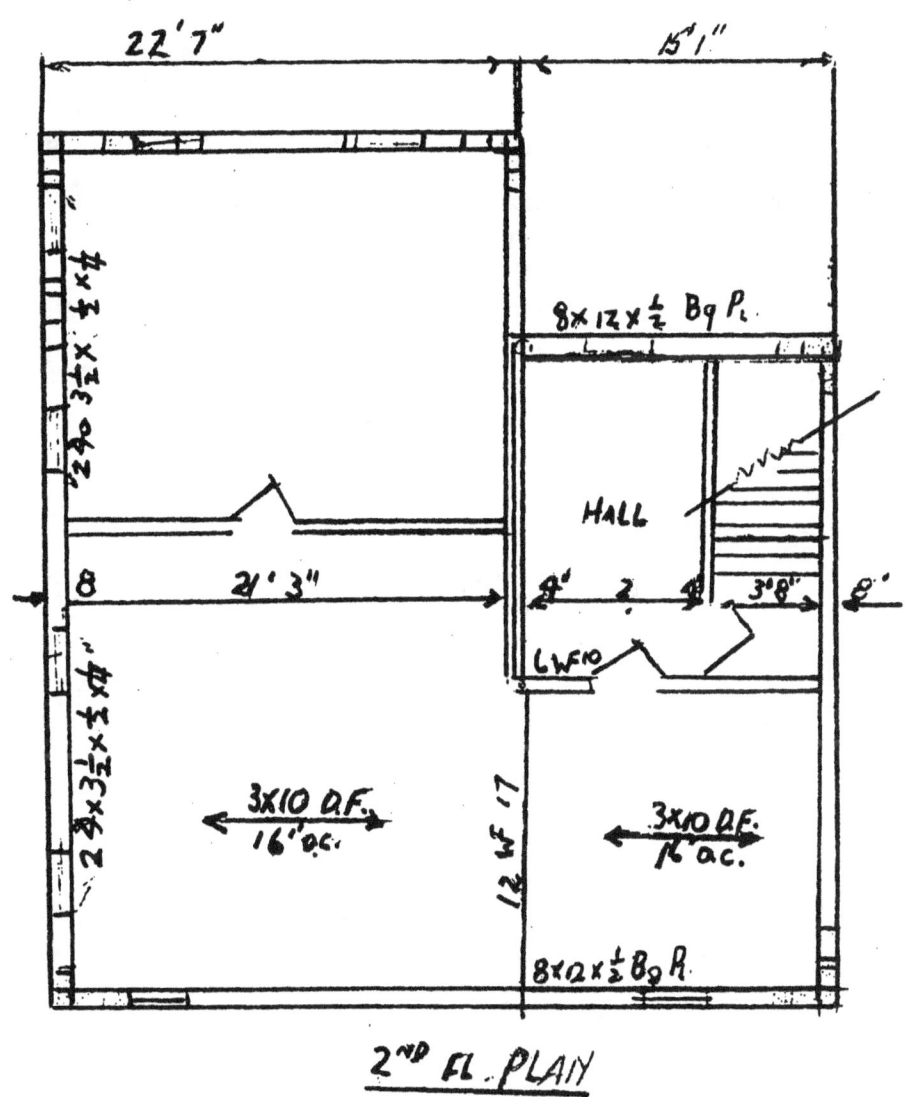

2ND FL. PLAN

46. The one of the following statements that is CORRECT is the building 46.____

   A. is of fireproof construction
   B. has masonry walls with wood joists
   C. is of wood frame construction
   D. has timber joists and girders

47. The one of the following statements that is CORRECT is   47._____

    A. the stairway from the ground continues through the roof
    B. there are two means of egress from the second floor of this building
    C. the door on the second floor stair landing opens in the direction of egress
    D. the entire stair is shown on this plan

48. The width of the hall is   48._____

    A. 10'3"   B. 10'5"   C. 10'7"   D. 10'9"

49. The lintels shown are   49._____

    A. angles
    C. an I-beam
    B. a channel and an angle
    D. precast concrete

50. The one of the following statements that is CORRECT is that the steel beam is   50._____

    A. supported by columns at the center and at the ends
    B. entirely supported by the walls
    C. supported on columns at the ends only
    D. supported at the center by a column and at the ends by the walls

---

KEY (CORRECT ANSWERS)

1. B	11. C	21. B	31. D	41. D
2. B	12. D	22. D	32. C	42. A
3. A	13. B	23. B	33. A	43. B
4. B	14. B	24. C	34. A	44. C
5. C	15. A	25. C	35. B	45. D
6. C	16. A	26. B	36. C	46. B
7. B	17. A	27. B	37. D	47. C
8. D	18. C	28. C	38. B	48. D
9. B	19. D	29. C	39. B	49. A
10. D	20. C	30. C	40. A	50. D

EXAMINATION SECTION
TEST 1

DIRECTIONS: Each question or incomplete statement is followed by several suggested answers or completions. Select the one that BEST answers the question or completes the statement. *PRINT THE LETTER OF THE CORRECT ANSWER IN THE SPACE AT THE RIGHT.*

1. A shrink fitted collar is to be removed from a shaft. One good way to do this would be to drive out the shaft after _____ collar.

    A. *chilling* only the
    B. *chilling* both the shaft and
    C. *heating* only the
    D. *heating* both the shaft and

2. It is CORRECT to say that

    A. a standard brick weighs about 8 lbs.
    B. the dimensions of a common brick are 8" x 3 3/4" x 2 1/4"
    C. vertical joints in a brick wall are called bed joints
    D. in laying bricks the head joints should be slushed with mortar

3. A snail pump impeller is checked for static balance by

    A. running the pump at high speed and listening for rubs
    B. mounting it on parallel and level knife edges and noting if it turns
    C. weighing it and comparing the weight against the original weight
    D. putting it on a lathe to see if it runs true

4. The sum of the following dimensions: 3' x 2 1/4", 8 7/8", 2'6 3/8", 2'9 3/4", and 1'0" is

    A. 16'7 1/4"   B. 10'7 1/4"   C. 10'3 1/4"   D. 9'3 1/4"

5. A requisition for nails was worded as follows: *100 lbs., 10d, 3 inch, common wive nails, galvanized.*
   The UNNECESSARY information in this requisition is

    A. 100 lbs.   B. common   C. galvanized   D. 3 inch

6. Electric arc welding is COMMONLY done by the use of _____ voltage and _____ amperage.

    A. low; high   B. high; high
    C. high; low   D. low; low

7. A GOOD principle for you to follow after teaching a maintenance procedure to a new helper is to

    A. tell him that you expect him to make many mistakes at first
    B. observe his work procedure and point out any errors he may make
    C. have him write out the procedure from memory
    D. assume he knows the procedure if he asks no questions

8. Multiple threads are used on the stems of some large valves to

   A. reduce the effort required to open the valve
   B. prevent binding of the valve stem
   C. secure faster opening and closing of the valve
   D. decrease the length of stem travel

9. After the base plate of a new machine has been fitted over the foundation bolts, it should be leveled by

   A. inserting steel shims under the plate
   B. chipping the high spots off the floor
   C. using thin cement grout under the plate
   D. grinding down the high spots on the base plate

10. In nixing concrete by hand, the materials are first thoroughly mixed dry and then mixed with water. This is a good procedure because it

    A. caves cement
    B. reduces the amount of water required
    C. avoids settling of the aggregate
    D. properly coats the aggregate with the cement

11. A revolution counter applied to the end of a rotating shaft reads 100 when a stopwatch is started and 850 after 90 seconds.
    The shaft is rotating at a speed of _____ rpm.

    A. 500   B. 633   C. 750   D. 950

12. If a kink develops in a wire rope, it would be BEST to

    A. hammer out the kink with a lead hammer
    B. straighten out the kink by putting it in a vise and applying sufficient pressure
    C. discard the portion of the rope containing the kink
    D. keep the rope in use and allow the kink to work itself out

13. Steel pipe posts have been placed into prepared holes in concrete.
    To properly secure the posts, they should be caulked inplace with

    A. molten lead   B. cement mortar
    C. oakum   D. hot pitch

14. The PRINCIPAL reason for grounding of electrical equipment is to

    A. save power   B. guard against shock
    C. prevent open circuits   D. prevent short circuits

15. A spirit level has been dropped and a deep indentation made in the wood.
    The BEST thing to do is to

    A. ignore the incident if the bubbles were not broken
    B. sand down the surface to remove the indentation
    C. get a new level
    D. test the level

16. A strike plate is MOST closely associated with a

    A. lock
    B. sash weight
    C. hinge
    D. door check

17. You receive a special assignment from your superior calling for the use of a type of wood which in your opinion is not suitable for the job.
    You should

    A. substitute the wood you believe to be most suitable
    B. carry out the order as received
    C. immediately call this to his attention
    D. consult another maintainer on what to do

18. A motor driven centrifugal pump takes water from a city main and delivers it to the nozzles of a train washing machine. With little change in motor speed or suction pressure, the discharge pressure rises and the flow of cleaning water falls to a trickle.
    The PROBABLE cause is a

    A. failure of the impeller shaft
    B. leak in the piping between the pressure gage point of attachment and the nozzles
    C. blockage of the impeller
    D. blockage between the pressure gage point of attachment and the nozzles

19. A standard hoisting rope size is designated as 6 x 19. This indicates that the rope has

    A. 6 strands, each made of 19 wires
    B. 19 strands, each made of 6 wires
    C. 6 strands of No. 19 gage wire
    D. 19 strands of No. 6 gage wire

20. The two planes which make up the MOST useful combination for general carpentry work are the _____ plane and the _____ plane.

    A. jack; jointer
    B. jack; block
    C. smooth; block
    D. fore; jointer

21. If you were drilling a structural plate and the drill cuttings were in the form of long continuous shavings, you could rightly conclude that the

    A. drill point was too sharp
    B. material being drilled was wrought iron
    C. bearing pressure on the drill was insufficient
    D. drilling was being done correctly

22. Studs and joists for light building construction are USUALLY spaced on _____ inch centers.

    A. 12   B. 14   C. 16   D. 18

23. If power driven rivets are loose, the MOST likely reason would be that the rivets were

    A. too long
    B. too short
    C. driven with high air pressure
    D. overheated

24. If a drawing for a pipe installation is made to a scale of 1 1/2" to the foot, the drawing is said to be one _____ size.

   A. half   B. quarter   C. eighth   D. sixteenth

25. A gear train consists of a driver with 120 teeth, an idler with 60 teeth, and a driven gear with 200 teeth. If the driver rotates at 1500 rpm, the driven gear rotates at _____ rpm.

   A. 225   B. 900   C. 2500   D. 10,000

26. A certain pipe fitting is marked *200 WOG*. This fitting could NOT properly be used in a pipe line for _____ pounds gage maximum.

   A. steam at 200   B. water at 150
   C. air at 200   D. oil at 150

27. A file having two *safe* edges is COMMONLY known as a _____ file.

   A. flat   B. mill   C. hand   D. pillar

28. By trial, it is found that by using 2 cubic feet of sand, a 5 cubic foot batch of concrete is produced.
   Using the same proportions, the amount of sand, in cubic feet, required to produce 2 cubic yards of concrete is MOST NEARLY

   A. 7   B. 22   C. 27   D. 45

29. Tooling of the face joints of a brick wall under construction should be done

   A. after the mortar has acquired its initial set
   B. after the entire wall is laid
   C. after the mortar has acquired its final set
   D. as each brick is laid

30. A gland bushing is associated in practice with a(n)

   A. gas engine   B. electric motor
   C. centrifugal pump   D. lathe

31. A house drain is successively offset by means of a 1/8 bend, a 1/16 bend, and a 1/32 bend.
   The total angular offset of this line is MOST NEARLY

   A. 34°   B. 39°   C. 68°   D. 79°

32. The flushing mechanism in a low tank water closet is so arranged that a fill tube supplies water from the ball cock to the overflow standpipe for a short interval immediately after the closet is flushed.
   The MAIN reason for this is to

   A. finish cleaning the water passages of the closet
   B. properly seal the ball in its seat
   C. renew the seal in the closet trap
   D. scour the flush tube from the tank to the closet

33. A job calls for the setting of wrought iron pipe sleeves in concrete floor construction for the passage of water risers.
    In order to provide for the passage of a 2" riser, the MINIMUM diameter of the sleeve is

    A. 2 1/2"   B. 3"   C. 4"   D. 5"

34. When applied to lumber, the designation *S4S* means

    A. all sides are rough
    B. all four sides are of the same size
    C. fourth grade lumber
    D. all sides are dressed

35. To guard against accidents in connection with wood scaffolding,

    A. inspect the nailing before the scaffold is loaded
    B. never put a heavy load on a scaffold
    C. use only heavy timber for scaffold construction
    D. do not build high scaffolds

36. A reducing tee has one run opening of 2 inches, the second run opening of 14 inches, and the branch opening of 1 inch.
    This tee would be specified as

    A. 1 x 1 1/2 x 2   B. 1 x 2 x 1 1/2
    C. 2 x 1 1/2 x 1   D. 2 x 1 x 1 1/2

37. A length of pipe is to be fitted with a 90° elbow at each end. The center to center distance between elbows is to be 4'6". The center to end dimension of each elbow is 2" and the thread engagement is 1/2".
    The length to which the pipe should be cut is

    A. 4'1"   B. 4'2"   C. 4'3"   D. 4'4 1/2"

38. Sheet metal seams are sometimes grooved. The MAIN function of the grooving is to

    A. facilitate making a soldered joint
    B. prevent unlocking
    C. improve the appearance of the joint
    D. save sheet metal

39. When fitting new piston rings in a compressor, the piston ring gap is BEST measured by means of a(n)

    A. feeler gage   B. inside caliper
    C. 6" rule   D. depth gage

40. The ampere-hour rating of a battery depends MAINLY on the

    A. number of cells connected in series
    B. casing composition
    C. quantity of electrolyte
    D. number and area of the battery plates

KEY (CORRECT ANSWERS)

1. C	11. A	21. D	31. D
2. B	12. C	22. C	32. C
3. B	13. A	23. B	33. B
4. C	14. B	24. C	34. D
5. D	15. D	25. B	35. A
6. A	16. A	26. A	36. C
7. B	17. C	27. D	37. C
8. C	18. D	28. B	38. B
9. A	19. A	29. A	39. A
10. D	20. B	30. C	40. D

TEST 2

DIRECTIONS: Each question or incomplete statement is followed by several suggested answers or completions. Select the one that BEST answers the question or completes the statement. *PRINT THE LETTER OF THE CORRECT ANSWER IN THE SPACE AT THE RIGHT.*

1. In making a high wooden scaffold, proper splices in 2 x 4 lumber which is to be used vertically would be made by   1.____

    A. lapping each joint with a cleat below
    B. butting the ends and boxing in the joints with 1" boards
    C. butting the ends and nailing a 2 x 4 over the splice
    D. making half-lap joints

2. With respect to soldering, it is LEAST important that   2.____

    A. the soldering copper be clean and well-tinned
    B. a good flux suitable for the metal being soldered be used
    C. the joint to be soldered be well-cleaned
    D. a lot of solder be used

3. When two sheet metal plates are riveted together, a specified minimum distance must be provided from the edge of each plate to the nearest line of rivets in order to prevent   3.____

    A. the rivet heads from working loose
    B. the rivets from being sheared
    C. tearing of the material between the rivets and the edges of the plates
    D. excessive stress on the rivets

4. A hoisting cable is wound on a 14" drum which is rotating at 5 rpm.
   The load being raised by this cable will move at an APPROXIMATE linear speed, in feet per minute, of   4.____

    A. 13.5   B. 18.3   C. 70   D. 220

5. Spreaders are used in connection with forms for concrete to   5.____

    A. hold the walls of a form the correct distance apart
    B. anchor a form to the ground
    C. make a form watertight
    D. make the cement spread evenly through the form

6. By curing of concrete is meant   6.____

    A. finishing the surface of the concrete
    B. softening stiff concrete by adding water
    C. keeping the concrete wet while setting
    D. the salvaging of frozen concrete

7. If steel weighs 480 lbs. per cubic foot, the weight of an 18" x 18" x 2" steel base plate is _____ lbs.   7.____

    A. 180   B. 216   C. 427   D. 648

8. Standard wrought iron pipe and extra strong wrought iron pipe of the same nominal size differ in

   A. outside diameter
   B. inside diameter
   C. chemical composition
   D. threading

9. Plunbing system stacks are vented to the atmosphere. These stacks will NOT

   A. relieve the back pressure on traps from the sewer side
   B. prevent the siphoning of traps
   C. ventilate the drainage system
   D. prevent the sewer from backing up into the fixtures

10. The MOST likely cause of accidents involving minor injuries is

    A. careless work practices
    B. lack of safety devices
    C. inferior equipment and material
    D. insufficient safety posters

11. In the maintenance of shop equipment, lubrication should be done

    A. periodically
    B. only if necessary
    C. whenever time permits
    D. only during the overhaul period

12. The total number of cubic yards of earth to be removed to nake a trench 3'9" wide, 25'0" long, and 4'3" deep is MOST NEARLY

    A. 53.1   B. 35.4   C. 26.6   D. 11.8

13. A large number of 2 x 4 studs, some 10'5" long and some 6'5 1/2" long, are required for a job.
    To minimize waste, it would be preferable to order lengths of _____ ft.

    A. 16   B. 17   C. 18   D. 19

14. A 6" pipe is connected to a 4" pipe through a reducer. If 100 cubic feet of water is flowing through the 6" pipe per minute, the flow, in cubic feet per minute, through the 4" pipe is

    A. 225   B. 100   C. 66.6   D. 44.4

15. The type of seam generally used in the construction of sheet metal cylinders of small diameters is the _____ seam.

    A. double edged
    B. folded
    C. double hemmed
    D. simple lap

16. Two branch ventilating ducts, one 12 inches square and the other 18 inches square, are to connect to a square main duct.
    In order to maintain the same cross-sectional area, the dimension of the main duct should be _____ inches square.

    A. 14   B. 20   C. 24   D. 28

17. In reference to preparing mortar, it is CORRECT to say that the lime used   17.____

    A. may burn the skin
    B. hastens setting
    C. prevents absorption of water by the brick
    D. decreases the amount of water needed

18. The intercooler of a two-stage air compressor is connected to the compressor unit   18.____

    A. before the air intake pipe to the first stage
    B. between the second stage and the receiver
    C. between the two stages
    D. after the receiver.

19. In oxyacetylene welding, the hose that is connected to the oxygen cylinder is USUALLY colored   19.____

    A. yellow   B. white   C. purple   D. green

20. When bonding new concrete to old concrete, the surface of the old concrete should be   20.____

    A. left untouched   B. dry
    C. carefully smoothed   D. chipped and roughened

21. A sack of Portland cement is considered to have a volume, in cubic feet, of   21.____

    A. 1/2   B. 3/4   C. 1   D. 14

22. The purpose of a vacuum breaker used with an automatic flush valve is to   22.____

    A. limit the flow of water to the fixture
    B. prevent pollution of the water supply
    C. equalize the water pressure
    D. control the water pressure to the fixture

23. Wiping solder for lead pipe USUALLY has a melting range of _____ °F.   23.____

    A. 150 to 250   B. 251 to 350
    C. 360 to 470   D. 475 to 600

24. A space heater is to be suspended from a structural beam. The heater should be suspended by a hanger   24.____

    A. passing through a hole in the web of the beam
    B. passing through a hole in the flange of the beam
    C. welded to the beam
    D. clamped to the beam

25. With respect to babbitted sleeve bearings, oil grooves are   25.____

    A. cut only on the top half
    B. cut only on the bottom half
    C. cut on both halves
    D. never necessary

26. When an employee finds it necessary to work near a live third rail, it is BEST to cover the third rail with a

   A. rubber mat B. canvas cloth
   C. board D. sheet of heavy paper

27. A 10-inch foundation wall is 11 feet long and 15 feet high. If the compressive strength of the wall is 300 pounds per square inch, the MAXIMUM permissible load on this wall is _____ lbs.

   A. 540,000 B. 495,000 C. 396,000 D. 33,000

28. It is INCORRECT to state that

   A. neat cement contains cement and water
   B. salt is used to hasten the setting of concrete
   C. the strength of concrete is affected by the water ratio
   D. a sidewalk should slope toward the street

29. When sharpening a hand saw, the FIRST operation is to file the teeth so that they are of the same height. This is known as

   A. shaping B. setting C. leveling D. jointing

30. The swing of a lathe is the

   A. diameter of the largest piece that can be turned
   B. distance between centers of the head and tail spindles
   C. size of the face plate
   D. radius of the chuck

31. Assume that the lead screw, stud gear, and spindle of a lathe revolve at the same speed. It is required to cut 10 threads per inch when the lead screw has 6 threads per inch. If the stud gear has 48 teeth, the lead screw gear must have _____ teeth.

   A. 48 B. 60 C. 64 D. 80

32. The safety device used on a crane to prevent overtravel is called a(n)

   A. unloader B. governor
   C. limit switch D. overload relay

33. It is INCORRECT to say that

   A. there is a difference between fittings for threaded drainage pipe and fittings for ordinary threaded pipe
   B. a gasoline torch must be fully filled with gasoline
   C. *Red Brass* pipe contains about 85% copper
   D. loose parts in a faucet may cause noisy operation

34. A requisition for lag screws does NOT require stating the

   A. diameter B. quantity
   C. threads per inch D. length

35. In an accident report, the information which may be MOST useful in decreasing the recurrence of similar type accidents is the

    A. extent of injuries sustained
    B. time the accident happened
    C. number of people involved
    D. cause of the accident

36. Carbon tetrachloride is NOT recommended for cleaning purposes because of

    A. the poisonous nature of its fumes
    B. its limited cleaning value
    C. the damaging effects it has on equipment
    D. the difficulty of application

37. The part of the thread directly measured with a thread micrometer is the

    A. thread height   B. major diameter
    C. thread lead   D. pitch diameter

38. The side support for steps or stairs is called a

    A. ledger board   B. runner
    C. stringer   D. riser

39. A sheet metal plate has been cut in the form of a right triangle with sides of 5, 12, and 13 inches.
    The area of this plate, in square inches, is

    A. 30   B. 32 1/2   C. 60   D. 78

40. The BEST first aid for a man who has no external injury but is apparently suffering from internal injury due to an accident is to

    A. take him at once to a doctor's office
    B. make him comfortable and immediately summon a doctor or ambulance
    C. administer a stimulant
    D. start artificial respiration

KEY (CORRECT ANSWERS)

1. B	11. A	21. C	31. D
2. D	12. D	22. B	32. C
3. C	13. C	23. C	33. B
4. B	14. B	24. D	34. C
5. A	15. D	25. A	35. D
6. C	16. B	26. A	36. A
7. A	17. A	27. C	37. D
8. B	18. C	28. B	38. C
9. D	19. D	29. D	39. A
10. A	20. D	30. A	40. B

EXAMINATION SECTION
TEST 1

DIRECTIONS: Each question or incomplete statement is followed by several suggested answers or completions. Select the one that BEST answers the question or completes the statement. *PRINT THE LETTER OF THE CORRECT ANSWER IN THE SPACE AT THE RIGHT.*

1. A bit is held in a hand drill by means of a(n)   1.____

   A. arbor   B. chuck   C. collet   D. clamp

2. The type of screw that MOST often requires a countersunk hole is a _____ head.   2.____

   A. flat   B. round   C. fillister   D. hexagon

3. Instead of using the ordinary 1 piece screwdriver, a screwdriver bit is MOST often used with a brace because of the   3.____

   A. increased length of the brace
   B. different types of bits available
   C. increased leverage of the brace
   D. ability to work in tight corners

4. A thread gage is usually used to measure the   4.____

   A. thickness of a thread
   B. diameter of a thread
   C. number of threads per inch
   D. height of a thread

5. The wheel of a glass cutter is BEST lubricated with   5.____

   A. kerosene
   B. linseed oil
   C. varnolene
   D. diesel oil

6. A nail set is a   6.____

   A. group of nails of the same size and type
   B. group of nails of different sizes but the same type
   C. tool used to extract nails
   D. tool used to drive nails below the surface of wood

7. To test for leaks in a gas line, it is BEST to use   7.____

   A. a match
   B. soapy water
   C. a colored dye
   D. ammonia

8. Routing is the process of cutting a   8.____

   A. strip out of sheet metal
   B. groove in wood
   C. chamfer on a shaft
   D. core out of concrete

9. A hacksaw frame has a wing nut mainly to   9.____

   A. make it easier to replace blades
   B. increase the strength of the frame
   C. prevent vibration of the blade
   D. adjust the length of the frame

10. A mitre box is usually used with a _____ saw. 10._____

    A. hack   B. crosscut   C. rip   D. back

11. A continuous flexible saw blade is MOST often used on a _____ saw. 11._____

    A. radial   B. band   C. swing   D. table

12. A pipe reamer is used to 12._____

    A. clean out a length of pipe
    B. thread pipe
    C. remove burrs from the ends of pipe
    D. seal pipe joints

13. To lay out a straight cut on a piece of wood at the same angle as the cut on a second piece of wood, the PROPER tool to use is a 13._____

    A. bevel   B. cope   C. butt gauge   D. clevis

14. Before drilling a hole in a piece of metal, an indentation should be made with a _____ punch. 14._____

    A. pin   B. taper   C. center   D. drift

15. Curved cuts in wood are BEST made with a _____ saw. 15._____

    A. jig   B. veneer   C. radial   D. swing

16. A face plate is generally used to 16._____

    A. hold material while working with it on a lathe
    B. smooth out irregularities in a metal plate
    C. protect the finish on a metal plate
    D. locate centers of holes to be drilled on a drill press

17. A die would be used to 17._____

    A. gage the groove in a splined shaft
    B. cut a thread on a metal rod
    C. hold a piece to be machined on a milling machine
    D. control the depth of a hole to be drilled in a piece of metal

18. Before using a ladle to scoop up molten solder, you should make sure that the ladle is dry. 18._____
This is done to prevent

    A. the solder from sticking to the ladle
    B. impurities from getting into the solder
    C. injuries due to splashing solder
    D. cooling of the solder

19. To PROPERLY adjust the gap on a spark plug, you should use a(n)

    A. inside caliper B. center gauge
    C. wire type feeler gauge D. micrometer

20. The length of the MOST common type of folding wood rule is _____ feet.

    A. 4 B. 5 C. 6 D. 7

21. A four-foot mason's level is usually used to determine whether the top of a wall is level and whether it is

    A. square B. plumb C. rigid D. in line

22. To match a tongue in a board, the matching board MUST have a

    A. rabbet B. chamfer C. bead D. groove

23. When driving screws in close quarters, the BEST type of screwdriver to use is a(n)

    A. Phillips B. offset C. butt D. angled

24. The term 12-24 refers to a _____ screw.

    A. wood B. lag
    C. sheet metal D. machine

25. To measure the length of a curved line on a drawing or plan, the PROPER tool to use in addition to a ruler is(are)

    A. dividers B. calipers
    C. surface gage D. radius gage

26. For the standard machine screw, the diameter of a tap drill is generally

    A. *equal* to the diameter of the shaft of the screw at the base of the threads (the root diameter)
    B. *larger* than the root diameter, but smaller than the diameter of the screw
    C. *equal* to the diameter of the screw
    D. *larger* than the diameter of the screw

27. In order to drill a 1" hole accurately with a drill press, you should

    A. drill at high speeds
    B. use very little pressure on the drill
    C. drill partway down, release pressure on the drill, and then continue drilling
    D. drill a pilot hole first

28. Before taking apart an electric motor to repair, punch marks are sometimes placed on the casing near each other.
    The MOST probable reason for doing this is to

    A. make sure the parts lock together on reassembly
    B. properly line up the parts that are next to each other
    C. keep track of the number of parts in the assembly
    D. identify all the parts as coming from the one motor

29. To locate a point on a floor directly under a point on the ceiling, the PROPER tool to use is a

   A. square
   B. line level
   C. height gage
   D. plumb bob

Question 30.

DIRECTIONS: Question 30 is based on the diagram appearing below.

30. In the above diagram, the full P required to lift the weight a distance of four feet is MOST NEARLY _____ lbs.

   A. 50   B. 67   C. 75   D. 100

31. The EASIEST tool to use to determine whether the edge of a board is at right angles to the face of the board is a

   A. rafter square
   B. try square
   C. protractor
   D. marking gage

32. *Whetting* refers to

   A. tempering of tools by dipping them in water
   B. annealing of tools by heating and slow cooling
   C. brazing of carbide tips on tools
   D. sharpening of tools

33. The MOST difficult part of a plank to plane is the

   A. face   B. side   C. end   D. back

34. To prevent wood from splitting when drilling with an auger, it is BEST to

   A. use even pressure on the bit
   B. drill at a slow speed
   C. hold the wood tightly in a vise
   D. back up the wood with a piece of scrap wood

35. The term *dressing a grinding wheel* refers to 35.____

   A. setting up the wheel on the arbor
   B. restoring the sharpness of a wheel face that has become clogged
   C. placing flanges against the sides of the wheel
   D. bringing the wheel up to speed before using it

36. Heads of rivets are BEST cut off with a 36.____

   A. hacksaw   B. cold chisel
   C. fly cutter   D. reamer

37. A *V-block* is especially useful to 37.____

   A. prevent damage to work held in a vise
   B. hold round stock while a hole is being drilled into it
   C. prevent rolling of round stock stored on the ground
   D. shim up the end of a machine so that it is level

38. A full set of taps for a given size usually consists of a _____ tap. 38.____

   A. taper and bottoming
   B. taper and plug
   C. plug and bottoming
   D. taper, plug, and bottoming

39. Round thread cutting dies are usually held in stock by means of 39.____

   A. wing nuts   B. clamps   C. set screws   D. bolts

40. The one of the following diagrams that shows the plan view and the elevation of a counterbored hole is 40.____

A.

B.

C.

D.

41. With regard to pipe, *I.D.* usually means 41.____

   A. inside diameter   B. inside dressed
   C. invert diameter   D. installation date

42. A compression fitting is MOST often used to 42.____

    A. lubricate a wheel
    B. join two pieces of tubing
    C. reduce the diameter of a hole
    D. press fit a gear to a shaft

43. The shape of a mill file is basically 43.____

    A. flat   B. half round   C. triangular   D. square

44. Of the following, the ratio of tin to lead that will produce the solder with the LOWEST melting point is 44.____

    A. 30-70   B. 40-60   C. 50-50   D. 60-40

45. A safe edge on a file is one that 45.____

    A. is smooth and can not cut
    B. has a finer cut than the face of the file
    C. is rounded to prevent scratches
    D. has a coarser cut than the face of the file

46. The MOST frequent use of a file card is to _____ files. 46.____

    A. sort out   B. clean
    C. prevent damage to   D. prevent clogging of

47. The BEST way of determining whether a grinding wheel has an internal crack is to 47.____

    A. run the wheel at high speed, stop it, and examine the wheel
    B. spray lubricating oil on the sides of the wheel and check the amount of absorption of the oil
    C. hit the wheel with a rubber hammer and listen to the sound
    D. drop the wheel sharply on a table and then check the wheel

48. If a grinding wheel has worn to a smaller diameter, the BEST practice to follow is to 48.____

    A. discard the wheel
    B. continue using the wheel as before
    C. use the wheel, but at a faster speed
    D. use the wheel, but at a slower speed

49. With respect to the ordinary awl, 49.____

    A. only the tip is hardened
    B. the entire blade is hardened
    C. the tip is tempered, and the rest of the blade is hardened
    D. the entire blade is tempered

50. To prevent overheating of drills, it is BEST to use _____ oil. 50.____

    A. cutting   B. lubricating
    C. penetrating   D. heating

KEY (CORRECT ANSWERS)

1. B	11. B	21. B	31. B	41. A
2. A	12. C	22. D	32. D	42. B
3. C	13. A	23. B	33. C	43. A
4. C	14. C	24. D	34. D	44. D
5. A	15. A	25. A	35. B	45. A
6. D	16. A	26. B	36. B	46. B
7. B	17. B	27. D	37. B	47. C
8. B	18. C	28. B	38. D	48. C
9. A	19. C	29. D	39. C	49. A
10. D	20. C	30. D	40. A	50. A

TEST 2

DIRECTIONS: Each question or incomplete statement is followed by several suggested answers or completions. Select the one that BEST answers the question or completes the statement. *PRINT THE LETTER OF THE CORRECT ANSWER IN THE SPACE AT THE RIGHT.*

1. Crocus cloth is commonly used to 1.____

   A. protect finely machined surfaces from damage while the machines are being repaired
   B. remove rust from steel
   C. protect floors and furniture while painting walls
   D. wipe up oil and grease that has spilled

2. Before using a new paint brush, the FIRST operation should be to 2.____

   A. remove loose bristles
   B. soak the brush in linseed oil
   C. hang the brush up overnight
   D. clean the brush with turpentine

3. When sharpening a hand saw, the FIRST operation is to 3.____

   A. file the teeth down to the same height
   B. shape the teeth to the proper profile
   C. bend the teeth over to provide clearance when sawing
   D. clean the gullies with a file

4. To prevent solder from dripping when soldering a vertical seam, it is BEST to 4.____

   A. hold a waxed rag under the soldering iron
   B. use the soldering iron in a horizontal position
   C. tin the soldering iron on one side only
   D. solder the seam in the order from bottom to top

5. If a round nut has two holes in the face, the PROPER type wrench to use to tighten this nut is a(n) 5.____

   A. Stillson   B. monkey   C. spanner   D. open end

6. A box wrench is BEST used on 6.____

   A. pipe fittings   B. flare nuts
   C. hexagonal nuts   D. Allen screws

7. To prevent damage to fine finishes on metal work that is to be held in a vise, you should 7.____

   A. clamp the work lightly
   B. use brass inserts on the vise
   C. wrap the work with cloth before inserting it in the vise
   D. substitute a smooth face plate for the serrated plate on the vise

8. The MOST frequent use for a turnbuckle is to

   A. tighten a guy wire
   B. adjust shims on a machine
   C. bolt a bracket to a wall
   D. support electric cable from a ceiling

9. To form the head of a tinner's rivet, the PROPER tool to use is a rivet

   A. anvil   B. plate   C. set   D. brake

10. A socket speed handle MOST closely resembles a

    A. screwdriver   B. brace   C. spanner   D. spin grip

11. Tips of masonry drills are usually made of

    A. steel   B. carbide   C. corundum   D. monel

12. The BEST flux to use for soldering galvanized iron is

    A. resin   B. sal ammoniac
    C. borax   D. muriatic acid

13. The one of the following that is NOT a common type of oilstone is

    A. silicon carbide   B. aluminum oxide
    C. hard Arkansas   D. pumice

14. A method of joining metals using temperatures intermediate between soldering and welding is

    A. corbelling   B. brazing   C. annealing   D. lapping

15. When an unusually high degree of accuracy is required with woodwork, lines should be marked with a

    A. pencil ground to a chisel point
    B. pencil line over a crayon line
    C. sharp knife point
    D. scriber

16. The MOST important difference between pipe threads and V threads on bolts is that pipe threads are usually

    A. longer   B. sharper
    C. tapered   D. more evenly spaced

17. A street elbow differs from the ordinary elbow in that the street elbow has

    A. different diameter threads at each end
    B. male threads at one end and female threads at the other
    C. female threads at both ends
    D. male threads at both ends

18. Water hammer in a pipe line can MOST often be stopped by the installation of a(n)

    A. pressure reducing valve   B. expansion joint
    C. flexible coupling   D. air chamber

19. If water is leaking from the top part of a bibcock, the part that should be replaced is MOST likely the

    A. bibb washer
    B. packing
    C. seat
    D. bibb screw

20. When joining electric wires together in a fixture box, the BEST thing to use are wire

    A. connectors   B. couplings   C. clamps   D. bolts

21. If the name plate of a motor indicates that it is a split phase motor, it is LIKELY that this motor

    A. is a universal motor
    B. operates on DC only
    C. operates on AC only
    D. operates either on DC at full power or on AC at reduced power

22. To make driving of a screw into hard wood easier, it is BEST to lubricate the threads of the screw with

    A. varnoline
    B. penetrating oil
    C. beeswax
    D. cutting oil

23. Assume that a thermostatically controlled oil heater fails to operate. To determine whether it is the thermostat that is at fault, you should

    A. check the circuit breaker
    B. connect a wire across the terminals of the thermostat
    C. replace the contacts on the thermostat
    D. put an ammeter on the line

24. The function of the carburetor on a gasoline engine is to

    A. mix the air and gasoline properly
    B. filter the fuel
    C. filter the air to engine
    D. pump the gasoline into the cylinder

25. If a car owner complains that the battery in his car is constantly running dry, the item that should be checked FIRST is the

    A. fan belt
    B. generator
    C. voltage regulator
    D. relay

26. On MOST modern automobiles, foot brake pressure is transmitted to the brake drums by

    A. air pressure
    B. mechanical linkage
    C. hydraulic fluid
    D. electro-magnetic force

27. Assume that the engine of a car remains cold even though it is run for a period of time. The part that is MOST likely at fault is the

    A. heat by-pass valve
    B. thermostat
    C. heater control
    D. choke

28. To permit easy stripping of concrete forms, they should be 28._____

   A. dried B. oiled C. wet down D. cleaned

29. To prevent honey combing in concrete, the concrete should be 29._____

   A. vibrated
   B. cured
   C. heated in cold weather
   D. protected from the rain

30. The MAIN reason for using wire mesh in connection with concrete work is to 30._____

   A. strain the impurities from the sand
   B. increase the strength of the concrete
   C. hold the forms together
   D. protect the concrete till it hardens

31. Segregation of concrete is MOST often caused by pouring concrete 31._____

   A. in cold weather
   B. from too great a height
   C. too rapidly
   D. into a form in which the concrete has already begun to harden

32. Headers in carpentry are MOST closely associated with 32._____

   A. trimmers
   B. cantilevers
   C. posts
   D. newels

33. Joists are very often supported by 33._____

   A. suspenders
   B. base plates
   C. anchor bolts
   D. bridal irons

34. At outside corners, the type of joint MOST frequently used on a baseboard is the 34._____

   A. plowed
   B. mitered
   C. mortise and tenon
   D. butt

35. The vehicle used with latex paints is usually 35._____

   A. linseed oil
   B. shellac
   C. varnish
   D. water

36. *Boxing* of paint refers to the _____ of paints. 36._____

   A. mixing B. storage C. use D. canning

37. When painting wood, nail holes should be puttied 37._____

   A. *before* applying the prime coat
   B. *after* applying the prime coat but before the second coat
   C. *after* applying the second coat but before the third coat
   D. *after* applying the third coat

38. In laying up a brick wall, you find that at the end of the wall there is not enough space for a full brick. 38._____
   You should use a

   A. stretcher B. bat C. corbel D. bull nose

39. Pointing a brick wall is the same as

   A. truing up the wall
   B. topping the wall with a waterproof surface
   C. repairing the mortar joints in the wall
   D. providing a foundation for the wall

40. The pigment MOST often used in a prime coat of paint on steel to prevent rusting is

   A. lampblack
   B. calcimine
   C. zinc oxide
   D. red lead

41. If you find a co-worker lying unconscious across an electric wire, the FIRST thing you should do is

   A. get him off the wire
   B. call the foreman
   C. get a doctor
   D. shut off the power

42.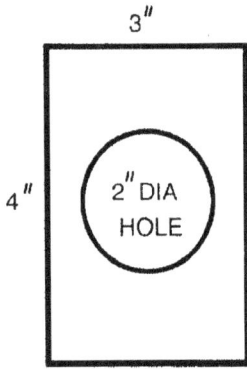

   The area of the metal plate shown above, minus the hole area, is MOST NEARLY _____ square inches.

   A. 8.5   B. 8.9   C. 9.4   D. 10.1

43.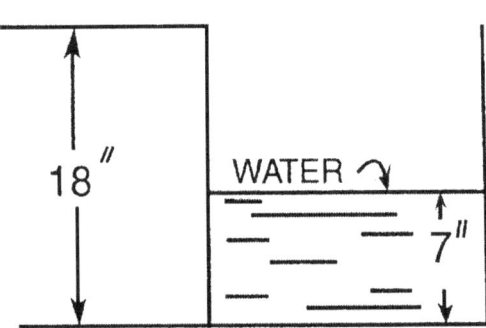

   The percentage of the above tank that is filled with water is MOST NEARLY

   A. 33   B. 35   C. 37   D. 39

44.

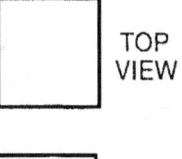

The top and front view of an object are shown above. The right side view will MOST likely look like

A.  B. 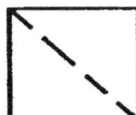 C. 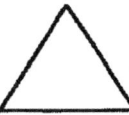 D.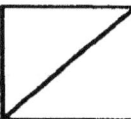

45.

The distance between centers of the holes in the above diagram is MOST NEARLY

A. $4\frac{1}{2}"$ B. 4 3/4"   C. 5"   D. $5\frac{1}{4}"$

Questions 46-48.

DIRECTIONS: Questions 46 through 48, inclusive, are to be answered in accordance with the paragraph below.

   A steam heating system with steam having a pressure of less than 10 pounds is called a low-pressure system. The majority of steam-heating systems are of this type. The steam may be provided by low-pressure boilers installed <u>expressly</u> for the purpose, or it may be gener-

ated in boilers at a higher pressure and reduced in pressure before admitted to the heating mains. In other instances, it may be possible to use exhaust steam which has been made to run engines and other machines and which still contains enough heat to be utilized in the heating system. The first case represents the system of heating used in the ordinary residence or other small building; the other two represent the systems of heating employed in industrial buildings where a power plant is installed for general power purposes.

46. According to the above paragraph, whether or not a steam heating system is considered a low pressure system is determined by the pressure

    A. generated by the boiler
    B. in the heating main
    C. at the inlet side of the reducing valve
    D. of the exhaust

47. According to the above paragraph, steam used for heating is sometimes obtained from steam

    A. generated principally to operate machinery
    B. exhausted from larger boilers
    C. generated at low pressure and brought up to high pressure before being used
    D. generated by engines other than boilers

48. As used in the above paragraph, the word *expressly* means

    A. rapidly   B. specifically
    C. usually   D. mainly

49. Of the following words, the one that is CORRECTLY spelled is

    A. suficient   B. sufficant
    C. sufficient   D. suficant

50. Of the following words, the one that is CORRECTLY spelled is

    A. fairly   B. fairley   C. farely   D. fairlie

KEY (CORRECT ANSWERS)

1. B	11. B	21. C	31. B	41. D
2. A	12. D	22. C	32. A	42. B
3. A	13. D	23. B	33. D	43. D
4. C	14. B	24. A	34. B	44. A
5. C	15. C	25. C	35. D	45. C
6. C	16. C	26. C	36. A	46. B
7. B	17. B	27. B	37. B	47. A
8. A	18. D	28. B	38. B	48. B
9. C	19. B	29. A	39. C	49. C
10. B	20. A	30. B	40. D	50. A

EXAMINATION SECTION
TEST 1

DIRECTIONS: Each question or incomplete statement is followed by several suggested answers or completions. Select the one that BEST answers the question or completes the statement. *PRINT THE LETTER OF THE CORRECT ANSWER IN THE SPACE AT THE RIGHT.*

Questions 1-8.

DIRECTIONS: Questions 1 through 8 involve tests on the fuse box arrangement shown below. All tests are to be performed with a neon tester or a lamp test bank consisting of two 6-watt, 120-volt lamps connected in series. Do not make any assumptions about the conditions of the circuits. Draw your conclusions only from the information obtained with the neon tester or the two-lamp test bank, applied to the circuits as called for.

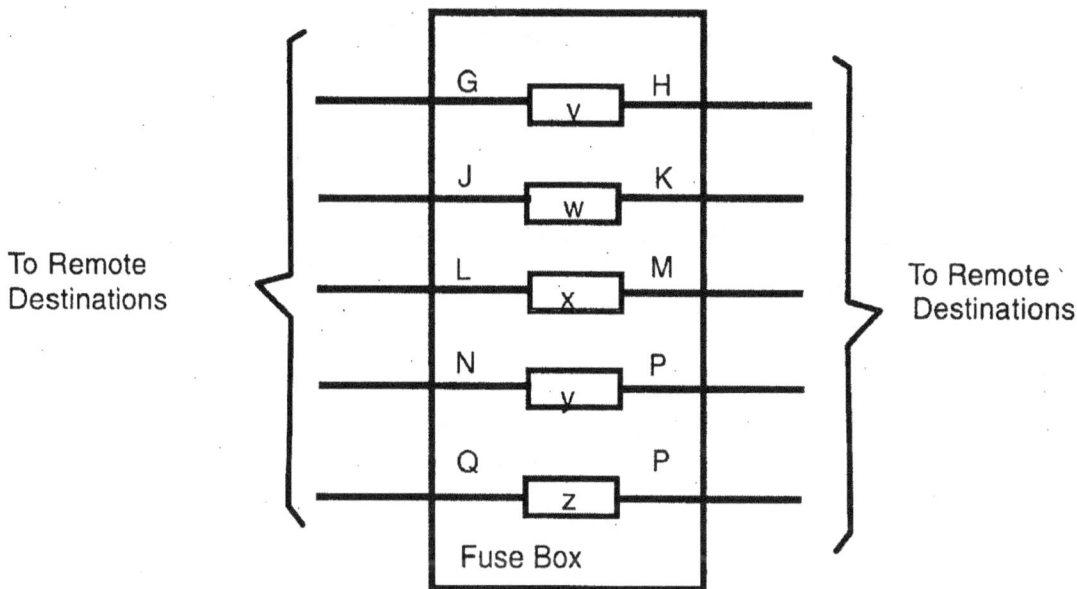

1. The two lamp test bank is placed from point *G* to joint *J*, and both lamps light. One of the lamps is momentarily removed from its socket; during that instant, the other lamp in the series-connected test bank should

   A. go dark
   B. get dimmer
   C. remain at same brightness
   D. get brighter

   1.____

2. The test bank with two 60-watt, 120-volt lamps in series should be used on circuits with

   A. wattages only from 60 to 120 watts
   B. wattages only from 0 to 120 watts
   C. voltages only from 120 to 240 volts
   D. voltages only from 0 to 240 volts

   2.____

77

3. The neon tester is placed from point G to point J and only one-half of the neon tester lights.
   It should be concluded that

   A. half of the tester has gone bad
   B. a wire has become disconnected in the circuit
   C. the voltage is AC
   D. the voltage is DC

   3.____

4. If both lamps in the test bank light when placed directly across one of the above fuses, it should be concluded that

   A. the fuse is good
   B. the fuse is blown
   C. the fuse is overrated
   D. further tests have to be made to determine the condition of the fuse

   4.____

5. If the lamp test bank does not light when placed directly across one of the above fuses, it should be concluded that

   A. the fuse is good
   B. the fuse is blown
   C. the fuse is overrated
   D. further tests have to be made to determine the condition of the fuse

   5.____

6. The lamp test bank lights when placed from point G to point J but does not light when placed from point H to point J.
   It should be concluded that

   A. the wire to point H has become disconnected
   B. the wire to point J has become disconnected
   C. fuse v is bad
   D. fuse w is bad

   6.____

7. The lamp test bank lights when placed from point L to point N but does not light when placed from point M to point P.
   It should be concluded that

   A. both fuses x and y are bad
   B. either fuse x or fuse y is bad or both are bad
   C. both fuses x and y are good
   D. these tests do not indicate the condition of any fuse

   7.____

8. The lamp test bank is placed from point L to point N, then from N to point Q, and finally from point L to point Q. In each case, both lamps light to full brightness.
   It should be concluded that points L, N, and Q have

   A. three-phase, 120 volts, AC, line-to-line
   B. plus and minus 120 volts, DC
   C. three-phase, 208 volts, AC
   D. plus and minus 240 volts, DC

   8.____

9. An automatic device used for regulating air temperature is a(n)

    A. rheostat   B. aquastat   C. thermostat   D. duostat

10. Assume that you have just completed a certain maintenance job which you feel is satisfactory, but your foreman asks you to make certain changes.
    The BEST procedure for you to follow is to

    A. request the foreman to assign this work to someone else
    B. have another maintainer verify that the job was done properly
    C. ask the foreman the reasons for the changes
    D. complain to the foreman's superior of this waste of time

11. The PROPER set of tools and equipment to be used to clean and adjust the ignition points of an automobile consists of a

    A. screwdriver, feeler gauge, and point file
    B. wrench, micrometer, and sandpaper
    C. scraper, micrometer, and emery cloth
    D. V-block, pliers, and sandpaper

12. The voltage developed in each cell of an automobile battery is _____ volts.

    A. 2   B. 4   C. 6   D. 12

13. The one of the following tools that is NOT used to clear plumbing stoppages is a

    A. force-cup   B. drain auger
    C. snake   D. pick-out iron

14. Eyebolts are generally fastened to the shells of machinery in order to

    A. act as a leveling device
    B. facilitate lifting
    C. permit easy tagging of the equipment
    D. reinforce the machine shells

15. When grinding a weld smooth, it is MOST important to avoid

    A. grinding too slowly
    B. overheating the surrounding metal
    C. grinding away too much of the weld
    D. grinding after the weld has cooled off

16. A cold chisel whose head has become *mushroomed* should NOT be used because

    A. it is impossible to hit the head squarely
    B. the chisel will not cut accurately
    C. chips might fly from the head
    D. the chisel has lost its *temper*

17. The type of screwdriver specially made to be used in tight spots is the

    A. Phillips   B. offset
    C. square shank   D. truss

18. An indication that a fluorescent lamp in a fixture should be replaced is

    A. humming in the fixture
    B. the ends of the lamp remain black when the lamp is lit
    C. poor or slow starting
    D. the lamp does not shut off each time the OFF button is pressed

19. Asbestos is used as a covering on electrical wires to provide protection from

    A. high voltage
    B. high temperatures
    C. water damage
    D. electrolysis

20. Many electric power tools, such as drills, have a third conductor in the line cord which should be connected to a grounded part of the power receptacle.
    The reason for this is to

    A. have a spare wire in case one power wire should break
    B. strengthen the power lead so that it cannot be easily damaged
    C. protect the user of the tool from electrical shocks
    D. allow use of the tool for extended periods of time without overheating

21. Employees are responsible for the good care, proper maintenance, and serviceable condition of the property issued or assigned for their use.
    As used above, *serviceable condition* means the property is in a state where it is

    A. capable of being repaired
    B. easily handled
    C. fit for use
    D. least expensive

22. A brush that has been used in shellac should be cleaned by washing it in

    A. water
    B. linseed oil
    C. lacquer thinner
    D. alcohol

23. Excessive moisture on a surface being painted would MOST likely result in

    A. alligatoring
    B. blistering
    C. cracking
    D. sagging

24. In order to reverse the direction of rotation of a series motor, the

    A. connections to the armature should be reversed
    B. connections to both the armature and the series field should be reversed
    C. connections of the motor to the power lines should be reversed
    D. series field should be placed in shunt with the armature

25. A megger is an instrument used to measure

    A. capacitance
    B. insulation resistance
    C. power
    D. illumination levels

26. The first aid treatment for chemical burns on the skin is

    A. treatment with ointment and then bandaging
    B. washing with large quantities of water and then treating as heat burns
    C. treatment with a neutralizing agent and no bandaging
    D. application of sodium bicarbonate and then bandaging

27. The chemical MOST frequently used to clean drains clogged with grease is 27._____

    A. muriatic acid B. soda ash
    C. ammonia D. caustic soda

28. When tapping a blind hole in a steel plate, the FIRST type of tap to use is a _____ tap. 28._____

    A. plug B. taper C. lead D. bottoming

29. A common handshaving tool used in woodwork is a(n) 29._____

    A. trammel B. router C. auger D. plane

30. *Dressing* a grinding wheel refers to 30._____

    A. making the wheel thinner
    B. replacing with a new wheel
    C. repairing a crack in the wheel
    D. making the wheel round

31. The maintainer who is MOST valuable is the one who 31._____

    A. offers to do the heavy lifting
    B. asks many questions about the work
    C. listens to instructions and carries them out
    D. makes many suggestions on work procedures

32. Of the following, turpentine is used for thinning 32._____

    A. latex paint B. red lead paint
    C. calcimine D. shellac

33. Of the following, the hacksaw blade BEST suited for cutting thin-walled tubing is one which has _____ teeth/inch. 33._____

    A. 14 B. 18 C. 24 D. 32

34. Because of its weather-resistant properties, a varnish commonly used on exterior surfaces is _____ varnish. 34._____

    A. spar B. flat C. rubbing D. hard oil

35. A trip spring or spring cylinder on a snow plow assembly is a device that 35._____

    A. absorbs the shock of impact when the plow strikes an obstacle in the road
    B. provides for snap-action in the lowering of the plow blade
    C. allows for quick removal or attachment of the snow plow supporting frame
    D. detaches the plow blade and lets it hang free when the plow blade is dragged backwards

36. The term *preventative maintenance* is used to identify a plan whereby 36._____

    A. equipment is serviced according to a regular schedule
    B. equipment is serviced as soon as it fails
    C. equipment is replaced as soon as it becomes obsolete
    D. all equipment is replaced periodically

37. The ratio of air to gasoline in an automobile engine is controlled by the

    A. gas filter
    B. fuel pump
    C. carburetor
    D. intake manifold

38. *Energizer* is another name given to the

    A. automobile battery
    B. fluorescent fixture ballast
    C. battery charger
    D. generator shunt field

39. Wearshoes may be found on

    A. circuit breakers
    B. automobile brake systems
    C. snow plows
    D. door sills

40. When moving heavy equipment by means of pipe rollers, it is MOST important to

    A. use solid steel rollers
    B. use rollers with different diameters
    C. see that the trailing roller does not slip out from under the equipment
    D. use more than three rollers at all times

41. The one of the following storage areas that is BEST for the storage of paint is one which is

    A. unheated and not ventilated
    B. cool and ventilated
    C. sunny and ventilated
    D. warm and not ventilated

42. The leverage that can be obtained with a wrench is determined mainly by the

    A. material of which the wrench is made
    B. gripping surface of the jaw
    C. length of the handle
    D. thickness of the wrench

43. A star drill is used to bore holes in

    A. steel   B. concrete   C. wood   D. sheet metal

44. The one of the following actions of a maintainer that is MOST likely to contribute to a good working relationship between him and his assistant is for him to

    A. observe the same rules of conduct that he expects his assistant to observe
    B. freely give advice on his assistant's personal problems
    C. always be frank and outspoken to his assistant in pointing out his faults
    D. expect his assistant to perform with equal efficiency on any job assigned

45. Three common types of windows are

    A. batten, casement, and awning
    B. batten, casement, and double-hung
    C. batten, double-hung, and awning
    D. casement, double-hung, and awning

46. A staircase has twelve risers, each 6 3/4" high. The TOTAL rise of the staircase is

   A. 6'2 1/4"   B. 6'9"   C. 7'0"   D. 7'3 3/4"

47. A twenty-foot straight ladder placed at an angle against a wall should be at a distance from the wall equal to _____ feet.

   A. 3   B. 5   C. 7   D. 9

48. Reflective sheeting traffic signs that have become dirty should be wiped with kerosene or gasoline FOLLOWED by a

   A. wiping with a soft cloth soaked in thin oil
   B. hand rub with very fine sandpaper
   C. wash with detergent and a rinse with water
   D. coating of shellac applied with a brush

49. A temporary wooden fence carrying red flags and built around an opening in a pavement to warn oncoming traffic is known as a

   A. batter board   B. bulkhead
   C. bollard   D. barricade

50. *Four-ply belted* is used to describe the construction of

   A. belt-drive pulleys
   B. auto tires
   C. electrical wiring insulation
   D. seat belts

KEY (CORRECT ANSWERS)

1. A	11. A	21. C	31. C	41. B
2. D	12. A	22. D	32. B	42. C
3. D	13. D	23. B	33. D	43. B
4. B	14. B	24. A	34. A	44. A
5. D	15. C	25. B	35. A	45. D
6. C	16. C	26. B	36. A	46. B
7. B	17. B	27. D	37. C	47. B
8. C	18. B	28. B	38. A	48. C
9. C	19. B	29. D	39. C	49. D
10. C	20. C	30. D	40. C	50. B

TEST 2

DIRECTIONS: Each question or incomplete statement is followed by several suggested answers or completions. Select the one that BEST answers the question or completes the statement. *PRINT THE LETTER OF THE CORRECT ANSWER IN THE SPACE AT THE RIGHT.*

1. An oil bath filter is MOST often used on a(n)

    A. air compressor
    B. auto engine
    C. electric generator
    D. steam boiler

2. A 3-ohm resistor placed across a 12-volt battery will dissipate _____ watts.

    A. 3 B. 4 C. 12 D. 48

3. Instead of using fuses, modern electric wiring uses

    A. quick switches
    B. circuit breakers
    C. fusible links
    D. lag blocks

4. The MOST common combination of gases used for welding is

    A. carbon dioxide and acetylene
    B. nitrogen and hydrogen
    C. oxygen and acetylene
    D. oxygen and hydrogen

5. If a wheel has turned through an angle of 180, then it has made _____ revolution(s).

    A. 1/4 B. 1/2 C. 1/8 D. 18

6. Sewer gas is prevented from backing up through a plumbing fixture by a

    A. water trap
    B. return elbow
    C. check valve
    D. float valve

7. Putty that is too stiff is made workable by adding

    A. gasoline
    B. linseed oil
    C. water
    D. lacquer thinner

8. A vertical wood member in the wall of a wood frame house is known as a

    A. A stringer
    B. ridge member
    C. stud
    D. header

9. A 10-to-1 step-down transformer has an input of 1 ampere at 120 volts AC. If the losses are negligible, the output of the transformer is _____ volts.

    A. 1 ampere at 12
    B. .1 ampere at 1200
    C. 10 amperes at 12
    D. 10 amperes at 120

10. An oscilloscope is an instrument used in

    A. measuring noise levels
    B. displaying waveforms of electrical signals
    C. indicating the concentrations of pollutants in air
    D. photographing high-speed events

11. Assume that a brake pedal of a truck goes to the floorboard when depressed. The one of the following that could cause this condition is

    A. a leak in the hydraulic lines
    B. a clogged hydraulic line
    C. scored drums
    D. glazed linings

12. The universal joints of an automobile are located on the

    A. suspension springs
    B. steering linkages
    C. wheel cylinders
    D. drive shaft

13. The MAIN purpose of a flexible coupling is to connect two shafts which are

    A. of different diameters
    B. of different shapes
    C. not in exact alignment
    D. of different material

14. When using a standard measuring micrometer, starting with a zero reading, one complete counterclockwise revolution of the sleeve will give a reading of _____ inch.

    A. .001   B. .010   C. .025   D. .250

15. If a nut is to be tightened to an exact specified value of inch-lbs., the wrench to use is a _____ wrench.

    A. spanner   B. box   C. lock-jaw   D. torque

16. Common permanent type anti-freezes for automobile cooling systems are MAINLY

    A. alcohol
    B. methanol
    C. ethylene glycol
    D. trychloroethylene

17. Plexiglas is also called

    A. mylar   B. lucite   C. isinglass   D. PVC

18. Long, curved lines are BEST cut in 1/4" plexiglas with a _____ saw.

    A. rip   B. jig   C. keyhole   D. coping

19. The specific gravity of storage battery cells can be measured with a(n)

    A. odometer   B. hydrometer   C. ammeter   D. dwell meter

20. A nail set is a tool used for

    A. straightening bent nails
    B. measuring nail sizes
    C. cutting nails to specified size
    D. driving a nail head into wood

21. To cut a number of 2" x 4" lengths of wood accurately at an angle of 45°, it is BEST to use a

    A. protractor   B. mitre-box   C. triangle   D. square

22. The type of fastener MOST commonly used when bolting to concrete uses a(n)   22.___
    A. expansion shield   B. U-bolt
    C. toggle bolt   D. turnbuckle

23. When an automobile engine does not start on a damp day, the trouble is MOST likely in the _____ system.   23.___
    A. ignition   B. cooling   C. fuel   D. lubricating

24. The battery of an automobile is prevented from discharging back through the alternator by the blocking action of the   24.___
    A. commutator   B. diodes   C. brushes   D. slip rings

25. The master cylinder in an automobile is actuated by the   25.___
    A. steering column   B. brake pedal
    C. clutch plate   D. cam shaft

26. The FINEST sandpaper from among the following is No.   26.___
    A. 3   B. 1   C. 2/0   D. 6/0

27. A screw whose head is buried below the surface of the wood that it is screwed into is said to be   27.___
    A. countersunk   B. scalloped
    C. expanded   D. flushed

28. The one of the following devices which is used to measure angles is the   28.___
    A. caliper   B. protractor
    C. marking gauge   D. divider

29. Before a new oil stone is used, it should be   29.___
    A. heated   B. soaked in oil
    C. coated with shellac   D. washed with soapy water

30. Dies are used for   30.___
    A. threading the outside ends of metal pipes
    B. making sweated joints on lead pipes
    C. cutting nipples to exact lengths
    D. caulking cast-iron pipe joints

31. The energy stored by a storage battery is commonly given in   31.___
    A. volts   B. amperes
    C. ampere-hours   D. kilowatts

32. *Vapor lock* occurs in automobile   32.___
    A. gas tanks   B. crankcases
    C. transmissions   D. carburetors

33. A woodworking tool used to bore odd-size holes for which there is no standard auger bit is a(n)

    A. single twist auger
    B. double twist auger
    C. expansive bit
    D. straight fluted drill

34. Soap is sometimes applied to wood screws in order to

    A. prevent rust
    B. make a tight fit
    C. make insertion easier
    D. prevent wood splitting

35. On a long run of copper tubing, the tubing is often bent in the shape of a horseshoe rather than being run in a straight line.
    The MAIN reason for this is to

    A. allow an excess that could be used in future repairs
    B. make it easier to install the tubing
    C. permit the tubing to expand and contract with changes in temperature
    D. eliminate the need for accurate measurements in cutting the tubing

36. Loss of seal water in a house water trap is prevented by the use of a

    A. drainage tee   B. faucet   C. hose bibb   D. vent

37. BX is a designation for a type of

    A. flexible armored electric cable
    B. flexible gas line
    C. rigid conduit
    D. electrical insulation

38. *WYE-WYE* and *DELTA-WYE* are two

    A. types of DC motor windings
    B. arrangements of 3-phase transformer connections
    C. types of electrical splices
    D. shapes of commutator bars

39. Green lumber should NOT be used in the building of scaffolding because it

    A. will not hold nails well
    B. easily splits when nailed
    C. may warp on drying
    D. is too expensive

40. *Scotchlite* ready-made traffic sign faces with heat-activated adhesive backings are applied to backing blanks by use of a

    A. temperature-controlled oven
    B. vacuum applicator
    C. hot water bath
    D. heated roller assembly

41. *Scotchcal* is a(n)

    A. reflective sheeting
    B. epoxy protective paint
    C. fluorescent film
    D. high temperature lubricant

42. Wooden ladders should NOT be painted because the paint 42.____

    A. is inflammable
    B. may cover defects in the wood
    C. makes the rungs slippery
    D. may deteriorate the wood

43. To prevent ladders from slipping, the bottoms of the ladder side rails are OFTEN fitted with 43.____

    A. automatic locks   B. ladder shoes
    C. ladder hooks   D. stirrups

44. A bowline is 44.____

    A. the sag that a scaffold develops when men get on it
    B. a knot with a loop that does not run
    C. a temporary telephone wire strung during emergencies
    D. the reference line established in ditch excavations

45. A method sometimes used to prevent a pipe from buckling during a bending operation is to 45.____

    A. bend the pipe very quickly
    B. keep the seam of the pipe on the outside of the bend
    C. nick the pipe at the center of the bend
    D. pack the inside of the pipe with sand

46. A rectifier changes 46.____

    A. DC to AC
    B. AC to DC
    C. single-phase power to three-phase power
    D. battery power to three-phase power

47. Continuity in a de-energized electrical circuit may be checked with a(n) 47.____

    A. voltmeter   B. ohmmeter   C. neon tester   D. rheostat

48. Of the following crankcase oils, the one that should be used in sub-zero weather is SAE 48.____

    A. 10W   B. 20W   C. 20   D. 30

49. Caster in an automobile is an adjustment in the 49.____

    A. ignition system   B. drive-shaft
    C. rear differential   D. front suspension

50. If the spark plugs in an engine run too hot, the result is MOST likely that 50.____

    A. oil and carbon compounds will accumulate on the insulators
    B. the electrodes will wear rapidly
    C. the timing will be retarded
    D. the ignition coil may become damaged

KEY (CORRECT ANSWERS)

1.	B	11.	A	21.	B	31.	C	41.	C
2.	B	12.	D	22.	A	32.	D	42.	B
3.	B	13.	C	23.	A	33.	C	43.	B
4.	C	14.	C	24.	B	34.	C	44.	B
5.	B	15.	D	25.	B	35.	C	45.	D
6.	A	16.	C	26.	D	36.	D	46.	B
7.	B	17.	B	27.	A	37.	A	47.	B
8.	C	18.	B	28.	B	38.	B	48.	A
9.	C	19.	B	29.	B	39.	C	49.	D
10.	B	20.	D	30.	A	40.	B	50.	B

EXAMINATION SECTION
TEST 1

DIRECTIONS: Each question or incomplete statement is followed by several suggested answers or completions. Select the one that BEST answers the question or completes the statement. *PRINT THE LETTER OF THE CORRECT ANSWER IN THE SPACE AT THE RIGHT.*

1. The composition of plumber's solder for wiping is APPROXIMATELY (ratio of tin to lead) 1.____

    A. 40-60 B. 50-50 C. 60-40 D. 70-30

2. A device used to lift sewage to the level of a sewer from a floor below the sewer grade is known as a(n) 2.____

    A. elevator B. ejector C. sump D. conveyer

3. A check valve in a piping system will 3.____

    A. permit excessive pressures in a boiler
    B. eliminate water hammer
    C. permit water to flow in only one direction
    D. control the rate of flow of water

4. The chemical MOST frequently used to clean drains clogged with grease is 4.____

    A. muriatic acid B. soda ash
    C. ammonia D. caustic soda

5. To test for leaks in a newly installed C.I. waste stack, 5.____

    A. oil of peppermint is poured into the top of the stack
    B. smoke under pressure is pumped into the stack
    C. a water meter is used to measure the water flow
    D. dye is placed in the system at the top of the stack

6. When installing a catch basin, the outlet should be located 6.____

    A. at the same level as the inlet
    B. above the inlet
    C. below the inlet
    D. at the invert

7. The copper float in a low down water tank is perforated so that water enters the ball. As a result, the tank will 7.____

    A. flush once, and then will not operate again
    B. not flush at all
    C. not flush completely
    D. continue to flush, but water will be wasted

8. If water leaks from the stem of a faucet when the faucet is opened, the _____ should be 8.____

    A. faucet; replaced B. cap nut; rethreaded
    C. seat; reground D. packing; replaced

9. In a hot water heating system, it may be necessary to *bleed* radiators to

   A. relieve high steam pressure
   B. permit entrapped, air to escape
   C. allow condensate to return to the boiler
   D. drain off waste water

10. When painting raw wood, puttying of nail holes should be done

    A. 24 hours before the prime coat
    B. immediately before the prime coat
    C. after the prime coat and before the second coat
    D. after the second coat and before the finish

11. In general, the one of the following that will dry *tack free* in the SHORTEST time is

    A. lacquer   B. varnish   C. enamel   D. oil paint

12. The *vehicle* MOST frequently used in paints for exterior wood surfaces is

    A. white lead   B. linseed oil
    C. japan   D. varnish

13. Painting of an interior plastered wall is usually delayed until the plaster is dry. If this practice is NOT followed, the paint might

    A. chalk   B. fade   C. run   D. blister

14. A *sealer* applied over knots and pitch streaks to prevent *bleeding* through paint is

    A. shellac   B. lacquer
    C. coal tar   D. carnauba wax

15. Painting of outside steel in near freezing (32° F) weather is poor practice MAINLY because

    A. the paint will not dry properly
    B. ice will form in the thinner
    C. more paint is required
    D. paint fumes are dangerous

16. When repainting exterior woodwork that has a glossy finish, good adhesion of paint is BEST obtained by first

    A. *washing* the work with diluted lye
    B. *dulling* the work with sandpaper
    C. *warming* the work with an electric heater
    D. *roughening* the work with a rasp

17. The one of the following methods of cleaning steelwork prior to painting that is NOT commonly used on exterior work, such as bridges, is

    A. sandblasting   B. flame cleaning
    C. wire brushing   D. pickling

18. When spraying oil paints, the type of gun and nozzle preferred is a _____ feed gun, _____ mix nozzle.

    A. pressure; internal
    B. pressure, external
    C. syphon; internal
    D. syphon; external

18.____

19. When opening a bag of cement, you find that the cement is lumpy.
    The cement should be

    A. discarded and not used at all
    B. crushed before placing in the mixer
    C. used as is since the mixer will grind it
    D. well mixed with water and stored overnight before using

19.____

20. A 1:2:4 concrete mix by volume is specified.
    If 6 cubic feet of cement is to be used in the mix, the volume of sand to use is, in cubic feet,

    A. 3
    B. 6
    C. 12
    D. 24

20.____

21. Honeycombing in concrete is BEST prevented by

    A. increasing water-cement ratio
    B. heating concrete in cold weather
    C. using mechanical vibrators
    D. adding calcium chloride

21.____

22. When a lightweight concrete is required, the one of the following that is COMMONLY used as an aggregate is

    A. gravel
    B. brick chips
    C. stone
    D. cinders

22.____

23. A rubbed finish on concrete is USUALLY obtained by use of a

    A. carborundum brick
    B. garnet sanding belt
    C. fibre brush and wax
    D. pad of steel wool

23.____

24. A copper strip is frequently embedded in the concrete across a construction joint in a concrete wall.
    The purpose of this is to

    A. make a watertight joint
    B. bond the two parts of the wall together
    C. prevent unequal settlement
    D. retard temperature cracking

24.____

25. In brickwork laid in common bond, a header course USUALLY occurs in every _____ course.

    A. 2nd
    B. 4th
    C. 6th
    D. 8th

25.____

26. Pointing of brickwork refers to

    A. cutting brick to fit
    B. patching mortar joints
    C. attaching brick veneer
    D. arranging brick in an arch

26.____

27. Furring is applied to brick walls to

    A. strengthen the wall
    B. waterproof the wall
    C. provide ventilation to prevent condensation
    D. provide a base for lathing

28. The FIRST coat in plaster work is *scratched* in order to

    A. remove excess plaster
    B. smooth the base for the second coat
    C. provide a bond for the second coat
    D. strengthen the base coat

29. An alloy used where resistance to corrosion is important is

    A. tungsten   B. mild steel   C. monel   D. tin

30. The size of iron pipe is given in terms of its nominal

    A. weight   B. inside diameter
    C. outside diameter   D. wall thickness

31. When preparing surfaces to be soldered, the FIRST step is

    A. tinning   B. sweating   C. heating   D. cleaning

32. To test for leaks in an acetylene torch, it is BEST that one use

    A. soapy water   B. a match
    C. a gas with a strong odor   D. a pressure gauge

33. One advantage of using a Pittsburgh lock seam when joining two pieces of sheet metal is that, once formed in the shop, it may be assembled anywhere with a

    A. hickey   B. swage   C. template   D. mallet

34. White cast iron is

    A. hard and brittle   B. hard and ductile
    C. ductile and malleable   D. brittle and malleable

35. The gage used for measuring copper wire is

    A. U.S. Standard   B. Stubbs
    C. Washburn and Moen   D. Brown and Sharpe

36. The BEST flux to use when soldering copper wires in an electric circuit is

    A. sal ammoniac   B. zinc chloride
    C. rosin   D. borax

37. The spark test, to determine the approximate composition of an unknown metal, is made by

    A. holding the metal against a grinding wheel
    B. striking flint on the unknown metal
    C. connecting wires from a source of electric power to the metal and striking an arc with a bare wire
    D. heating with an oxyacetylene torch

38. The one of the following metals that is MOST commonly used for bearings is

   A. duraluminum B. brass C. babbit D. lead

39. A *tailstock* is found on a

   A. drill press B. shaper C. planer D. lathe

40. The BEST lubricant to use when cutting screw threads in steel is

   A. naphtha B. 3-in-1 oil
   C. lard oil D. linseed oil

41. When a high speed cutting tool is required, the tip is frequently made of

   A. carborundum B. tungsten carbide
   C. bronze D. vanadium

42. A nut is turned on a 3/4"-10 bolt.
   When the nut is turned five complete turns on this bolt, the distance it moves along the bolt

   A. depends on the type of thread B. is 0.2 inches
   C. is 0.375 inches D. is 0.5 inches

43. Of the following, the STRONGEST screw thread form is the

   A. Whitworth B. Acme
   C. National Standard D. V

44. *Knurling* refers to

   A. rolling depressions in a fixed pattern on a cylindrical surface
   B. turning between centers on a lathe
   C. making deep cuts in a flat plate with a milling machine
   D. drilling matching holes in bolt and nut for a cotter pin

45. A special device used to guide the drill as well as to hold the work when drilling is known as a

   A. dolly B. jig C. chuck D. collet

46. Tools that have a *Morse taper* would be used on a

   A. milling machine B. shaper
   C. planer D. drill press

47. When tapping a blind hole in a plate, the FIRST tap to use is a

   A. plug B. bottoming C. lead D. taper

48. An important safety practice to remember when cutting a rivet with a chisel is to wear

   A. leather gloves B. steel toe shoes
   C. cup goggles D. a hard hat

49. Electricians working around *live wires* should wear gloves made of 49.____

    A. asbestos   B. metal mesh   C. leather   D. rubber

50. Storage of oily rags presents a safety hazard because of possible 50.____

    A. fire   B. poisonous flames
    C. attraction of rats   D. leakage of oil

KEY (CORRECT ANSWERS)

1. A	11. A	21. C	31. D	41. B
2. B	12. B	22. D	32. A	42. D
3. C	13. D	23. A	33. D	43. B
4. D	14. A	24. A	34. A	44. A
5. B	15. A	25. C	35. B	45. B
6. C	16. B	26. B	36. C	46. D
7. D	17. D	27. D	37. A	47. D
8. D	18. A	28. C	38. C	48. C
9. B	19. A	29. C	39. D	49. D
10. C	20. C	30. B	40. C	50. A

TEST 2

DIRECTIONS: Each question or incomplete statement is followed by several suggested answers or completions. Select the one that BEST answers the question or completes the statement. *PRINT THE LETTER OF THE CORRECT ANSWER IN THE SPACE AT THE RIGHT.*

1. *Shimmying* of the front wheels of a truck is MOST frequently caused by 1.____

    A. worn front brake drums
    B. a worn differential gear
    C. a loose steering gear
    D. a dead shock absorber

2. The MOST important reason for maintaining correct air pressure in all tires of a truck is to 2.____

    A. prevent the truck from swerving when brakes are applied
    B. permit the truck to stop quicker in an emergency
    C. provide a smoother ride
    D. prevent excessive wear on the tires

3. The oil gage on the dashboard of a truck indicates 3.____

    A. the amount of oil in the pan
    B. the pressure at which the oil is being pumped
    C. if the oil filter is working
    D. the temperature of the oil in the motor

4. An unbalanced wheel on a truck is corrected by 4.____

    A. bending the rim slightly
    B. adjusting the king pin
    C. changing the ratio of caster to camber
    D. adding small weights to the rim

5. A cold motor on a truck should be warmed up in wintertime by 5.____

    A. turning on the heater and pouring warm water into the radiator
    B. allowing the motor to idle for a few minutes
    C. racing the motor
    D. alternately pressing the gas pedal to the floor and releasing it

6. The brake pedal on a truck goes to the floorboard when pushed. The one of the following that would cause this condition is 6.____

    A. air in the hydraulic system
    B. wet brakes
    C. excessive fluid in the cylinders
    D. a loose backing plate

7. The ammeter of a truck indicates no charge during operation even though the battery is run down. To find the fault, the generator field terminal is grounded. The ammeter now shows a charge. The part that is defective is the 7.____

    A. generator field coil
    B. armature
    C. brushes
    D. voltage regulator

8. The part used to control the ratio of air and gasoline in a truck engine is the

   A. bogie   B. filter   C. carburetor   D. pump

9. The MAIN purpose of a vacuum booster on a truck engine is to

   A. increase the manifold vacuum
   B. assist windshield wiper operation
   C. provide a steadier fuel flow
   D. govern engine speed

10. The purpose of grounding the frame of an electric motor is to

    A. prevent excessive vibration
    B. eliminate shock hazards
    C. reduce power requirements
    D. prevent overheating

11. The one of the following that is NOT part of an electric motor is a

    A. brush   B. rheostat   C. pole   D. commutator

12. An electrical transformer would be used to

    A. change current from AC to DC
    B. raise or lower the power
    C. raise or lower the voltage
    D. change the frequency

13. The piece of equipment that would be rated in ampere hours is a

    A. storage battery
    B. bus bar
    C. rectifier
    D. capacitor

14. A ballast is a necessity in a(n)

    A. motor generator set
    B. fluorescent lighting system
    C. oil circuit breaker
    D. synchronous converter

15. The power factor in an AC circuit is on when

    A. no current is flowing
    B. the voltage at the source is a minimum
    C. the voltage and current are in phase
    D. there is no load

16. Neglecting the internal resistance in the battery, the current flowing through the battery shown in the sketch above is _____ amp.

    A. 3   B. 6   C. 9   D. 12

17. When excess current flows, a circuit breaker is opened directly by the action of a

    A. condenser   B. transistor   C. relay   D. solenoid

18. The MAIN purpose of bridging in building floor construction is to

    A. spread floor loads evenly to joists
    B. reduce the number of joists required
    C. permit use of thinner subflooring
    D. reduce noise passage through floors

19. Of the following, the material MOST commonly used for subflooring is

    A. rock lath   B. insulation board
    C. plywood   D. transite

20. In connection with stair construction, the one of the following that is LEAST related to the others is

    A. tread   B. cap   C. nosing   D. riser

21. The type of nail MOST commonly used in flooring is

    A. common   B. cut   C. brad   D. casing

22. The edge joint of flooring boards is COMMONLY

    A. mortise and tenon   B. shiplap
    C. half lap   D. tongue and groove

23. The purpose of a ridge board in building construction is to

    A. locate corners of a building
    B. keep plaster work smooth
    C. support the ends of roof rafters
    D. conceal openings at the eaves

24. To prevent splintering of wood when using an auger bit,

    A. the bit should be hollow ground
    B. hold the piece of wood in a vise
    C. clamp a piece of scrap wood to the back of the piece being drilled
    D. use a slow speed on the drill press

25. End grain of a post can be MOST easily planed by use of a _____ plane.

    A. rafter   B. jack   C. fore   D. block

26. A butt gauge is used when

    A. hanging doors   B. laying out stairs
    C. making rafter cuts   D. framing studs

27. The one of the following grades of sandpaper with the FINEST grit is

    A. 0   B. 2/0   C. 1/2   D. 1

28. The sum of the following numbers, 3 7/8, 14 1/4, 6 7/16, 22 3/16, 8 1/2 is   28.____

    A. 55 1/16   B. 55 1/8   C. 55 3/16   D. 55 1/4

29. The area of the rectangular field shown in the diagram at the right is, in square feet,   29.____

    A. 29,456
    B. 29,626
    C. 29,716
    D. 29,836

(Diagram: rectangle, 437 FT. by 68 ft)

30. The cost of material is approximately 3/8ths of the total cost of a certain job. If the total cost of the job is $127.56, then the cost of material is MOST NEARLY   30.____

    A. $47.83   B. $48.24   C. $48.65   D. $49.06

31. A blueprint is drawn to a scale of 1/4" = 1'0". A line on the blueprint that is not dimensioned is measured with a ruler and found to be 3 3/8" long.
The length represented by this line is   31.____

    A. 13'2"   B. 13'4"   C. 13'6"   D. 13'8"

32. A maintainer, in repairing a brick wall, spends one-half hour getting materials, forty-three minutes chipping and cleaning the wall, fifteen minutes mixing the mortar, and one hour and twenty-seven minutes in applying the brick and finishing.
The total time spent on this repair job is _____ hours _____ minute(s).   32.____

    A. 2; 45   B. 2; 50   C. 2; 55   D. 3; 0

33. *Employees are responsible for the good care, proper maintenance, and serviceable condition of property issued or assigned to their use.*
As used above, *serviceable condition* means MOST NEARLY   33.____

    A. capable of being repaired   B. fit for use
    C. ease of handling   D. minimum cost

34. An employee shall be on the alert constantly for potential accident hazards.
As used above, *potential* means MOST NEARLY   34.____

    A. dangerous   B. careless   C. possible   D. frequent

Questions 35-37.

DIRECTIONS: Questions 35 to 37, inclusive, are to be answered in accordance with the following paragraph.

All cement work contracts, more or less, in setting. The contraction in concrete walls and other structures causes fine cracks to develop at regular intervals. The tendency to contract increases in direct proportion to the quantity of cement in the concrete. A rich mixture will contract more than a lean mixture. A concrete wall, which has been made of a very lean mixture and which has been built by filling only about one foot in depth of concrete in the form each day will frequently require close inspection to reveal the cracks.

35. According to the above paragraph,

    A. shrinkage seldom occurs in concrete
    B. shrinkage occurs only in certain types of concrete
    C. by placing concrete at regular intervals, shrinkage may be avoided
    D. it is impossible to prevent shrinkage

36. According to the above paragraph, the one of the factors which reduces shrinkage in concrete is the

    A. volume of concrete in wall
    B. height of each day's pour
    C. length of wall
    D. length and height of wall

37. According to the above paragraph, a rich mixture

    A. pours the easiest
    B. shows the largest amount of cracks
    C. is low in cement content
    D. need not be inspected since cracks are few

Questions 38-39.

DIRECTIONS: Questions 38 and 39 are to be answered in accordance with the following paragraph.

Painting is done to preserve surfaces, and unless the surface is properly prepared, good preservation will not be possible. Apply paint only to clean dry surfaces. After a surface has been scaled, which means that all loose paint and rust are removed by chipping, scraping, and wire brushing, be sure all dust and dirt are completely removed.

38. According to the above paragraph, the MAIN purpose of painting a wall is to _____ the wall.

    A. clean
    B. waterproof
    C. protect
    D. remove dust from

39. According to the above paragraph,

    A. chipping, scraping, and wire brushing are the only methods permitted for cleaning surfaces
    B. painting is effective only when the surface is clean
    C. scaling refers only to the removal of rust
    D. paint may be applied on wet surfaces

40. The order in which the dimensions of stock are listed on a bill of materials is

    A. thickness, length, and width
    B. thickness, width, and length
    C. width, length, and thickness
    D. length, thickness, and width

41. The glue that will BEST withstand extreme exposure to moisture and water is _____ glue.

    A. polyvinyl
    B. resorcinol
    C. powdered resin
    D. protein

42. Four board feet of lumber, listed at $350.00 per M, will cost

    A. $3.50   B. $1.40   C. $1.30   D. $4.00

43. The cap iron or chip breaker stiffens the plane iron and

    A. protects the cutting edge
    B. curls the shaving
    C. regulates the thickness of the shaving
    D. reduces mouth gap

44. Coping-saw blades have teeth shaped like those on a _____ saw.

    A. dovetail   B. crosscut   C. back   D. rip

45. Of the following, the claw hammer that is BEST suited for general use in a woodworking shop is the _____ claw.

    A. straight
    B. bell-faced curved
    C. plain-faced curved
    D. adze eye curved

46. The natural binder which cements wood fibers together and makes wood solid is

    A. cellulose
    B. lignin
    C. alpha-cellulose
    D. trichocarpa

47. The plane that is BEST suited for trimming the bottom of a dado or lap joint is the _____ plane.

    A. block   B. router   C. rabbet   D. core-box

48. Brads are fasteners that are similar to _____ nails.

    A. escutcheon
    B. box
    C. finishing
    D. duplex head

49. The plane in which the plane iron is inserted with its bevel in the up position is the _____ plane.

    A. fore   B. rabbet   C. block   D. circular

50. Coating materials used to protect wood against fire USUALLY contain a water soluble fire-retardant such as

    A. ammonium chloride
    B. sodium perborate
    C. sodium silicate
    D. sal soda

KEY (CORRECT ANSWERS)

1. C	11. B	21. B	31. C	41. B
2. D	12. C	22. D	32. C	42. B
3. B	13. A	23. C	33. B	43. B
4. D	14. B	24. C	34. C	44. D
5. B	15. C	25. D	35. D	45. B
6. A	16. A	26. A	36. B	46. B
7. D	17. D	27. B	37. B	47. B
8. C	18. A	28. D	38. C	48. C
9. B	19. C	29. C	39. B	49. C
10. B	20. B	30. A	40. B	50. C

EXAMINATION SECTION
TEST 1

DIRECTIONS: Each question or incomplete statement is followed by several suggested answers or completions. Select the one that BEST answers the question or completes the statement. *PRINT THE LETTER OF THE CORRECT ANSWER IN THE SPACE AT THE RIGHT.*

1. Assume that a supervisor finds that his employees have become fatigued from doing a very long and repetitious job.
   The one of the following which would be the BEST way to relieve this fatigue is to
   A. assign other work so that the employees can switch to different assignments in the middle of the day
   B. let the employees listen to a radio while they work
   C. break the job down into very small parts so that each employee can concentrate on one simple task
   D. allow the employees to take frequent rest periods

   1.____

2. Assume that one of your subordinates is injured and will be out for at least six weeks.
   Of the following, the BEST way to handle the work normally assigned to this person is to
   A. allow the work to remain uncompleted until the injured person returns, since he is the one who can BEST do this work
   B. divide this work equally among the persons under your supervision who can do this work
   C. do all the work yourself
   D. give the injured person's work to the most efficient member of your staff

   2.____

3. Suppose that another supervisor tells you about a new way to organize some of your unit's work. The idea sounds good to you. However, before you were in this unit, a similar plan was tried and it failed.
   The MOST important thing for you to do FIRST is to
   A. find out why the previous attempt failed
   B. suggest that the other supervisor tell his idea to top management
   C. try the plan to see whether it works
   D. find proof that the plan has worked elsewhere

   3.____

4. One of your subordinates comes to you with a grievance. You discuss it with him so that you may fully understand the problem as he sees it. However, since you are uncertain as to the proper answer, you should
   A. tell him that you cannot help him with this problem
   B. tell him that you will have to check further and make an appointment to see him again
   C. send him to see your immediate superior for a solution to the problem
   D. ask him to find out from his co-workers whether this problem has come up before

   4.____

5. A supervisor reprimanded one of his subordinates severely for making a serious error in judgment while performing an assignment for which he had volunteered.
   The supervisor's action was
   A. *incorrect*, chiefly because in the future the worker will probably try to avoid taking on responsibility
   B. *correct*, chiefly because this will insure that the worker will not make the same mistake in the future
   C. *correct*, chiefly because the worker should be discouraged from using his own judgment on the job
   D. *incorrect*, chiefly because the reprimand came too late to correct the error that had already been made

6. Of the following, the BEST way for a supervisor to inform all his subordinates of a change in lunch rules is, in MOST cases, to
   A. call a staff meeting
   B. tell each one individually
   C. issue a memorandum
   D. tell one or two employees to pass the word around

7. For a supervisor to assign work giving only general instructions to his subordinate would be advisable when
   A. the supervisor is confident that the worker knows how to do the job
   B. the assignment is a simple one
   C. the subordinate is himself a supervisory employee
   D. errors in the work will not cause serious delay

8. One of the DISADVANTAGES of setting minimum standards of performance for custodial employees is that
   A. such standards eliminate the basis for evaluating employees
   B. the custodial employees may keep their performance at the minimum level
   C. standards are always subject to change
   D. the supervisor may feel that his initiative is being restricted

9. One of your subordinates has been functioning below his usual level. You feel that something of a personal nature may be affecting his work. When you ask him casually whether anything is wrong, he says everything is fine.
   As a next step, it would be BEST to
   A. make frequent casual and humorous comments about the poor quality of his work but refrain, at this time, from any serious discussion
   B. warn him that failure to maintain his customary level of performance might result in disciplinary action
   C. express your concern privately and reveal your interest in the reason for his change in work performance
   D. discuss with him the work of another employee, suggesting that the other employee would be a good example to follow

3 (#1)

10. Assume you are teaching a new job to one of your subordinates. After you have demonstrated the job, you can BEST maintain the worker's interest by
    A. showing him training films about the job
    B. giving him printed material that explains why the job is important
    C. having him observe other workers do the job
    D. letting him attempt to do the job by himself under supervision

10.____

11. *Insubordination is sometimes a protest against inferior or arbitrary leadership.*
    For the supervisor, the MOST basic implication of the above statement is:
    A. Accusations of insubordination are easy to make, but usually difficult to prove.
    B. Insubordination cannot be permitted if an organization wishes to remain effective.
    C. When an employee discusses an order instead of carrying it out, he has not understood it.
    D. When an employee questions an order, review it to make sure it is reasonable.

11.____

12. In appraising a subordinate's mistakes, a supervisor should ALWAYS consider the
    A. absolute number of mistakes, without regard to severity
    B. number of mistakes in proportion to the number of decisions made
    C. total number of mistakes made by other, regardless of assignment
    D. number of mistakes which were discovered upon higher review

12.____

13. If you are the supervisor of an office in which the work frequently involves lifting heavy boxes, you should instruct your staff in the proper method of lifting to avoid injury.
    In giving these instructions, you should stress that a person lifting heavy objects MUST
    A. keep his feet close together
    B. bend at the waist
    C. keep his back as straight as possible
    D. use his back muscles to straighten up

13.____

14. Of the following, the BEST qualified supervisor is one who
    A. knows the basic principles and procedures of all the jobs which he supervises
    B. has detailed working knowledge of all aspects of the job he supervises but knows little about principles of supervision
    C. is able to do exceptionally well at least one of the jobs which he supervises and as some knowledge of the others
    D. knows little or nothing about most of the jobs which he supervises but knows the principles of supervision

14.____

15. The rate at which an employee will learn will vary according to a number of considerations.
    Of the following, which is LEAST likely to be controllable by the supervisor or the trainer? The
    A. manner in which the material is presented
    B. state of readiness of the learner
    C. scheduling of practice sessions
    D. nature of the material

16. When considering whether to use written material rather than oral instructions as a means of giving instructions to employees, the one of the following which should be given GREATEST consideration is the employees'
    A. personal preferences
    B. attitude toward supervision
    C. general educational level
    D. salary level

17. Assume that one of your subordinates has been assigned to attend job training classes.
    The one of the following which would probably be the BEST evidence of the success of the course is that the employee
    A. feels that he has learned something
    B. continues to study after the course is over
    C. has had a good class record
    D. improves in his work performance

18. Of the following, the situation LEAST likely to result if a supervisor shows favoritism toward particular employees is
    A. laxity in the work of the favored employees
    B. resentment from the other, less-favored employees
    C. increased ability among the favored employees
    D. lowering of morale among employees

19. The one of the following reasons for evaluating employees' performance, whether done formally or informally, which is NOT considered to be POSITIVE in nature is to
    A. give individual counsel to employees
    B. motivate employees toward improvement
    C. provide recognition of superior service
    D. set penalties for substandard performance

20. Assume that, because there has been an unexpected and temporary increase in the short-term work of your unit, you have had temporarily assigned to you several staff members from another agency.
    Of the following, in dealing with these employees, it would be LEAST advisable to
    A. assign them to long-term projects
    B. organize tasks so that they can begin work immediately
    C. set standards, making allowances to give them time to learn your ways
    D. direct them in the same way, in general, as you do your regular staff

21. It has been suggested that one way to increase employee productivity would be to require employees dealing with the public to have proficiency in a relevant foreign language.
Of the following, the MAJOR reason for implementing such a proposal, from the viewpoint of effective public administration, would be to
    A. encourage the foreign-born to learn English
    B. exchange information more rapidly and accurately
    C. increase the public prestige of the agency
    D. stimulate ethnic pride among all groups

21.____

22. Assume that the clerk who normally keeps your unit's records will be on vacation for four weeks.
If other clerks are equally qualified to keep these records, your BEST choice to replace the clerk would be the person who
    A. has skills which are needed least for other duties during this period
    B. volunteers for this work
    C. is next in turn for a special assignment
    D. has handled this task before

22.____

23. Assume that you have under your supervision several young clerical employees who have the bad habit of fooling around when they should be working.
Of the following, the BEST disciplinary action to take would be to
    A. ignore it; these young people will outgrow it
    B. join in the fun briefly in order to bring it to a quicker end each time it occurs
    C. bring to their attention the fact that this behavior is not acceptable and if it continues shift the make-up of the group to keep these young persons apart
    D. warn them that this type of behavior is reason for dismissal and be quick to make an example of the first one who starts it again

23.____

24. Seeking the advice of community leaders has human relations value for a public agency in planning or executing its programs CHIEFLY because it
    A. allows for the keeping of careful records concerning individual suggestions
    B. lets community leaders know that the agency has regard for their opinions
    C. permits the agency to state in writing which programs seem most appropriate
    D. unifies community leaders against the programs of competing private agencies

24.____

25. Good community relations is often action-oriented.
Which of the following activities of a public agency is LEAST likely to be considered as action-oriented by the people of a local community?
    A. Conducting a survey to gather information about the local community
    B. Extending the use of a facility to those previously excluded
    C. Providing a service that was formerly non-existent
    D. Removing something considered objectionable by the local community

25.____

KEY (CORRECT ANSWERS)

1. A
2. B
3. A
4. B
5. A

6. C
7. A
8. B
9. C
10. D

11. D
12. B
13. C
14. A
15. B

16. C
17. D
18. D
19. D
20. A

21. B
22. A
23. C
24. B
25. A

TEST 2

DIRECTIONS: Each question or incomplete statement is followed by several suggested answers or completions. Select the one that BEST answers the question or completes the statement. *PRINT THE LETTER OF THE CORRECT ANSWER IN THE SPACE AT THE RIGHT.*

1. Methods of communication with employees are of three types: oral, written, and visual.
   A MAJOR advantage of the written word is that it
   A. insures that content will remain unchanged no matter how many persons may be involved in its transmission
   B. facilitates two-way communication in delicate or confidential situations
   C. strengthens chain-of-command procedures in transmission of information and instruction by requiring the use of prescribed channels
   D. encourages the active participation of employees in the solution of complicated problems

   1.____

2. The use of the conference technique in training often requires more preparatory work on the part of the trainer than does a good lecture PRIMARILY because
   A. a conference would cover material of a more technical nature
   B. the trainer will be required to supply more printed material to the participants
   C. a conference usually involves a greater number of trainees
   D. the trainer must be prepared for a wide variety of possible occurrences

   2.____

3. The one of the following which is NOT an advantage of the lecture over most other methods of training is that it can be given
   A. over the radio or on record
   B. to large numbers of trainees
   C. without interruptions
   D. with little preparation

   3.____

4. Of the following, the one which is LEAST appropriate as a purpose for using an employee attitude survey is to
   A. develop a supervisory training program
   B. learn the identity of dissatisfied employees
   C. re-evaluate employee relations policies
   D. re-orient publications designed for employees

   4.____

5. The competent trainer seeks to become knowledgeable both in the work of the agency and in the duties of the positions for which he is to conduct training. Of the following, the GREATEST practical value that result when the trainer gains such knowledge is that
   A. he will be more likely to instruct employees to perform their work in a manner consistent with actual practice
   B. all levels of staff will be favorably impressed by a display of interest in the agency and its work
   C. employees will become familiar with the trainer and will not consider him an outsider
   D. the trainer will gain an accurate picture of the capacity of each employee for training

   5.____

6. Assume that you, the supervisor of a small office, are involved in planning the reorganization of your bureau's work. Management has decided not to inform your staff of the reorganization until the plans are completed.
   If one of your subordinates tells you that he has heard a rumor about reorganization of the department, you should reply that
   A. the reorganization involves the bureau, not the department
   B. you haven't heard anything about departmental reorganization and that he should stop spreading rumors
   C. you will inform your staff at the appropriate time if any definite plans are made involving a reorganization
   D. you do not know what is being planned but will ask your superior for details

6._____

7. Of the following training methods, the one in which the trainee's role is usually LEAST active is the _____ method.
   A. case-study   B. conference
   C. group discussion   D. lecture

7._____

8. Differences in morale between two work groups can sometimes be attributed to differences in the supervision they receive.
   Of the following, the behavior MOST characteristic of a supervisor of a group with high morale is that he
   A. assigns the least difficult tasks to employees with the most seniority
   B. is concerned primarily with his ultimate responsibility, production
   C. delegates authority and responsibility to his staff
   D. is lenient with his workers when they violate rules

8._____

9. Informal performance evaluations of individual employees, prepared systematically and regularly over a period of several years, are considered to be useful to a supervisor PRIMARILY because
   A. he will be able to assign tasks based only on these records
   B. unlike formal records, since they are fitted to the characteristics of individual employees, they provide for quick comparisons
   C. he need not discuss them with employees, since they are informal
   D. whatever personnel action he recommends can be substantiated by cumulative records

9._____

10. When instructing first-line supervisors in the proper method of evaluating the performance of probationary employees, it is LEAST important for a higher-level supervisor to
    A. explain in detail the standards to be used
    B. inform them of the possibility of higher management review
    C. caution them concerning common errors of evaluation
    D. mention the purposes of probationary employee evaluation

10._____

11. Assume that your agency is considering abolishing its official performance rating system but that you, a supervisor of a fairly large office, would like to devise a system for your own use.
    The FIRST step in setting up a system would be to
    A. decide what factors and personal characteristics are important and should be rated
    B. compare several rating methods to see which would be easiest to use
    C. have a private conference with each employee to discuss his performance
    D. set specific standards of employee performance, allowing your workers to make suggestions

12. The basic organizational structure of a municipal agency may have come about for several reasons.
    Of the following, the MOST important influence on the nature of its structure is the agency's
    A. professional attitude
    B. public reputation
    C. overall goal
    D. staff morale

13. The term *formal organization* refers to that organization structure agreed upon by top management whereas the term *informal organization* refers to the more spontaneous and flexible organizational ties developed by subordinates.
    The one of the following which BEST describes the usual *informal organization* is that it represents a(n)
    A. destructive system of relationships which should be eliminated
    B. concealed system of relationships whose goals are the same as management's
    C. actual system of relationships which should be recognized
    D. dysfunctional system of relationships which should be ignored

14. The reluctance of supervisors to delegate work to subordinates when they should is GENERALLY due to the supervisor's
    A. feelings of insecurity in work situations
    B. need to acquire additional experience
    C. inability to exercise control over his subordinates
    D. lack of technical knowledge

15. Assume that you have just been made the supervisor of a group of people you did not know before.
    For you to talk casually with each of your new subordinates with the purpose of getting to know them personally would be
    A. *advisable*, chiefly because subordinates have more confidence in a supervisor who shows personal interest in them
    B. *inadvisable*, chiefly because subordinates resent having their supervisor ask about their outside interests
    C. *advisable*, chiefly because one of the supervisor's main concerns should be to help his subordinates with their personal problems
    D. *inadvisable*, chiefly because a supervisor should not allow his relations with his subordinates to be influenced by their personalities

16. It has been found that high-producing subdivisions of organizations usually have supervisors whose behavior is employee-centered, whereas low-producing units usually have supervisors whose behavior is work-centered.
Therefore, it could be concluded from these findings that
    A. a high-producing unit may cause a supervisor to be authoritarian
    B. a low-producing unit may cause a supervisor to be work-centered
    C. close supervision usually increases production
    D. employee-centered leadership may reduce production

17. A recent study in managerial science showed that, as the amount of praise increased and amount of criticism decreased, the supervisor was more likely to be perceived by his subordinates as being
    A. concerned with their career advancement
    B. production oriented, through subtle intimidation
    C. seeking personal satisfaction, irrespective of production
    D. uncertain of the subordinates' reliability

18. The power to issue directives or instructions to employees is derived from employees as much as from management.
It follows MOST logically from this statement that
    A. attitudes toward management can be changed
    B. emphasis on discipline is needed
    C. authority is dependent upon acceptance
    D. employees should be properly supervised for work to be done

19. "In the decision-making process, it is a rare problem that has only one possible solution. Such a solution should be suspected of being nothing but a plausible argument for a preconceived idea."
The author of the foregoing quotation apparently does NOT believe that
    A. there is usually only one possible solution to a problem
    B. the risks involved in any solution should be weighed against expected gains
    C. each alternative should be evaluated to determine the effort needed
    D. actions should be based on the urgency of problems

20. The supervisor who relies on punitive discipline to enforce his authority is putting limits on the potential of his leadership. Fear of punishment may secure obedience, but it destroys initiative. Such a supervisor's autocratic methods have cut off upward communications.
Of the following, the major DISADVANTAGE of such autocratic behavior is that
    A. difficulties in the supervision of his subordinates will arise if limits are placed on the supervisor's responsibility
    B. policies that affect the public will be changed too frequently
    C. the supervisor will apply punishment subjectively rather than objectively
    D. instructions will be obeyed to the letter, regardless of changing circumstances

21. The need for a supervisor to carefully coordinate and direct the work of his unit increases as the work becomes
    A. more routine
    B. more specialized
    C. less complex
    D. less technical

    21.____

22. The MAIN goal of discipline as used by a supervisor should be to
    A. keep the employees' respect
    B. influence behavior, so that work will be completed properly
    C. encourage the employees to work faster
    D. set an example for others

    22.____

23. One of your subordinates has exhibited discourtesy and non-cooperation on several occasions.
    Of the following, the MOST appropriate attitude for you to adopt in dealing with this problem is that
    A. disciplinary measures for such an individual generally creates additional problems
    B. failure to correct such behavior may lead to worse offenses
    C. it is a mistake to make an issue out of minor infractions
    D. the harsher the medicine, the faster the cure

    23.____

24. Assume that an employee has complained to you, his supervisor, that he cannot concentrate on his work because two of his co-workers make too much noise. You pay particular attention to these employees for several days and do not find them making excessive noise.
    The NEXT step you should take in handling this grievance is to
    A. have a talk with all three employees, urging them to cooperate and be considerate of one another
    B. arrange for the complainant to change his work location to a place away from the two co-workers
    C. talk to the complainant to find out if the complaint he made to you is the real cause of his dissatisfaction
    D. tell the complainant that you have found his grievance to be unfounded

    24.____

25. In planning the application of an existing agency program to a local community, it is generally necessary to discover relevant problems and possibilities for service.
    Of the following, the BEST way to learn about such problems and possibilities for service would usually be to
    A. begin the program on a full-scale basis and await reactions
    B. seek opinions and advice from community residents and leaders
    C. hold staff meetings with agency employees who have worked in similar communities
    D. study official federal reports about already completed programs of the same kind

    25.____

KEY (CORRECT ANSWERS)

1. A
2. D
3. D
4. B
5. A

6. C
7. D
8. C
9. D
10. B

11. A
12. C
13. C
14. A
15. A

16. B
17. A
18. C
19. A
20. D

21. B
22. B
23. B
24. C
25. B

TEST 3

DIRECTIONS: Each question or incomplete statement is followed by several suggested answers or completions. Select the one that BEST answers the question or completes the statement. *PRINT THE LETTER OF THE CORRECT ANSWER IN THE SPACE AT THE RIGHT.*

1. Which of the following characteristics would be LEAST detrimental to a supervisor in his efforts to set up and maintain good relations with other supervisors with whom he must deal in the course of his duties?
   A. Not getting involved in consultation on any supervisory problems they might have
   B. Indicating that they should improve their supervising methods and offering suggestions on how to do so
   C. Emphasizing his own role as a member of management
   D. Sharing information which has proved useful in his unit

   1.____

2. Both trainers and supervisors might agree that there is usually a best way to do a particular job. Yet a supervisor or instructor sometimes does not teach a new employee the best way, the most efficient way, to do a complex job.
   Sometimes, in such cases, the supervisor temporarily changes the sequence of operations, increases the number of steps needed to do a job, or makes other changes in the method, which then deviates from the one considered most efficient.
   When is such a difference in approach MOST justified when teaching a new employee a complex job?
   A. When the changes in approach correspond to the learning ability of the new employee
   B. When the new employee's performance on the job is closely supervised to compensate for a change in approach
   C. Where the steps in performing the task have not been defined in a manual of procedures
   D. When the instructor has ideas of improving upon the methods for doing the job

   2.____

3. Considerable thought in the field of management is directed toward the advantages and disadvantages of authoritarian methods of influencing behavior, and, in the so-called authoritarian model, a nucleus of rather consistent ideas prevail.
   Which of the following is LEAST characteristic of an administrative system based on the authoritarian model?
   A. A conviction of a need for order and efficiency in a world consisting mainly of people who lack direction and incentive
   B. Rules and contracts are the basis for action, and decisions are made on an impersonal basis
   C. The right to give orders and instructions is inherent in the hierarchical arrangement of an organizational structure
   D. Realization that subordinates' needs for affiliation and recognition can contribute to management's objectives

   3.____

4. Of the following, the FIRST step in planning an operation is to 4.____
   A. obtain relevant information
   B. identify the goal to be achieved
   C. consider possible alternatives
   D. make necessary assignments

5. A supervisor who is extremely busy performing routine tasks is MOST likely 5.____
   making incorrect use of what basis principle of supervision?
   A. Homogeneous Assignment
   B. Span of Control
   C. Work Distribution
   D. Delegation of Authority

6. Controls help supervisors to obtain information from which they can determine 6.____
   whether their staffs are achieving planned goals.
   Which one of the following would be LEAST useful as a control device?
   A. Employee diaries
   B. Organization charts
   C. Periodic inspections
   D. Progress charts

7. A certain employee has difficulty in effectively performing a particular portion 7.____
   of his routine assignments, but his overall productivity is average.
   As a direct supervisor of this individual, your BEST course of action would be to
   A. attempt to develop the investigator's capacity to execute the problematical facets of his assignments
   B. diversify the investigator's work assignments in order to build up his confidence
   C. reassign the investigator to less difficult tasks
   D. request in a private conversation that the investigator improve his work output

8. A supervisor who uses persuasion as a means of supervising a unit would 8.____
   GENERALLY also use which of the following practices to supervise his unit?
   A. Supervises and control the staff with an authoritative attitude to indicate that he is a *take-charge* individual
   B. Make significant changes in the organizational operations so as to improve job efficiency
   C. Remove major communication barriers between himself, subordinates, and management
   D. Supervise everyday operations while being mindful of the problems of his subordinates

9. Whenever a supervisor in charge of a unit delegates a routine task to a capable 9.____
   subordinate, he tells him exactly how to do it.
   This practice is GENERALLY
   A. *desirable*, chiefly because good supervisors should be aware of the traits of their subordinates and delegate responsibilities to them accordingly
   B. *undesirable*, chiefly because only non-routine tasks should be delegated
   C. *desirable*, chiefly because a supervisor should frequently test the willingness of his subordinates to perform ordinary tasks
   D. *undesirable*, chiefly because a capable subordinate should usually be allowed to exercise his own discretion in doing a routine job

10. The one of the following activities through which a supervisor BEST demonstrates leadership ability is by
    A. arranging periodic staff meetings in order to keep his subordinates informed about professional developments in the field of investigation
    B. frequently issuing definite orders and directives which will lessen the need for subordinates to make decisions in handling any investigations assigned to them
    C. devoting the major part of his time to supervising subordinates so as to stimulate continuous improvement
    D. setting aside time for self-development and research so as to improve the investigative techniques and procedures of his unit

11. The following three statements relate to supervision of employees:
    I. The assignment of difficult tasks that offer a challenge is more conducive to good morale than the assignment of easy tasks.
    II. The same general principles of supervision that apply to men are equally applicable to women.
    III. The best restraining program should cover all phases of an employee's work in a general manner.
    Which of the following choices lists ALL of the above statements that are generally CORRECT?
    A. II, III   B. I   C. I, II   D. I, II, III

12. Which of the following examples BEST illustrates the application of the *exception principle* as a supervisory technique? A(n)
    A. complex job is divided among several employees who work simultaneously to complete the whole job in a shorter time
    B. employee is required to complete any task delegated to him to such an extent that nothing is left for the superior who delegated the task except to approve it
    C. superior delegates responsibility to a subordinate but retains authority to make the final decisions
    D. superior delegates all work possible to his subordinates and retains that which requires his personal attention or performance

13. Assume that you are a supervisor. Your immediate superior frequently gives orders to your subordinates without your knowledge.
    Of the following, the MOST direct and effective way for you to handle this problem is to
    A. tell your subordinates to take orders only from you
    B. submit a report to higher authority in which you cite specific instances
    C. discuss it with your immediate superior
    D. find out to what extent you authority and prestige as a supervisor have been affected

14. In an agency which has as its primary purpose the protection of the public against fraudulent business practices, which of the following would GENERALLY be considered an auxiliary or staff rather than a line function?

A. Interviewing victims of frauds and advising them about their legal remedies
B. Daily activities directed toward prevention of fraudulent business practices
C. Keeping records and statistics about business violations reported and corrected
D. Follow-up inspections by investigators after corrective action has been taken

15. A supervisor can MOST effectively reduce the spread of false rumors through the *grapevine* by
    A. identifying and disciplining any subordinate responsible for initiating such rumors
    B. keeping his subordinates informed as much as possible about matters affecting them
    C. denying false rumors which might tend to lower staff morale and productivity
    D. making sure confidential matters are kept secure from access by unauthorized employees

15.____

16. A supervisor has tried to learn about the background, education, and family relationships of his subordinates through observation, personal contact, and inspection of their personnel records.
    These supervisory actions are GENERALLY
    A. *inadvisable*, chiefly because they may lead to charges of favoritism
    B. *advisable*, chiefly because they may make him more popular with his subordinates
    C. *inadvisable*, chiefly because his efforts may be regarded as an invasion of privacy
    D. *advisable*, chiefly because the information may enable him to develop better understanding of each of his subordinates

16.____

17. In an emergency situation, when action must be taken immediately, it is BEST for the supervisor to give orders in the form of
    A. direct commands, which are brief and precise
    B. requests, so that his subordinate will not become alarmed
    C. suggestions, which offer alternative courses of action
    D. implied directive, so that his subordinates may use their judgment in carrying them out

17.____

18. When demonstrating a new and complex procedure to a group of subordinates, it is ESSENTIAL that a supervisor
    A. go slowly and repeat the steps involved at least once
    B. show the employees common errors and the consequences of such errors
    C. go through the process at the usual speed so that the employees can see the rate at which they should work
    D. distribute summaries of the procedure during the demonstration and instruct his subordinates to refer to them afterwards

18.____

19. The PRIMARY value of office reports and procedures is to
    A. assist top management in controlling key agency functions
    B. measure job performance
    C. save time and labor
    D. control the activities and use of time of all staff members

    19.____

20. Of the following, which is considered to be the GREATEST advantage of the oral report? It
    A. allows for accurate transmission of information from one individual to another
    B. presents an opportunity to discuss or clarify any immediate questions raised by the receiver of the report
    C. requires less office work to maintain records on actions taken when an oral report is involved
    D. takes only a short amount of time to plan and prepare material for an oral report

    20.____

21. A supervisor who is to make a report about a job he has done can make an oral report of a written report.
    Of the following, which is the BEST time to make an oral report? When
    A. the work covers an emergency situation
    B. a record is needed for the files
    C. the report is channeled to other departments
    D. the report covers additional work he will do

    21.____

22. Suppose that a new employee has been assigned to you. It is your responsibility to see to it that he understands how to fill out properly the forms he is required to use.
    What would be the BEST way to do this?
    A. Explain the use of each form to the new technician and show him how to fill them out
    B. Give the new employee a copy of each form he must use so that he can learn by studying them
    C. Ask an experienced worker to explain clearly to him how the forms should be filled out
    D. Tell the new employee that filling out forms is simple and he should follow the instructions on each form

    22.____

23. As a supervisor, you want to have your staff take part in improving work methods.
    Of the following, the BEST way to do this is to
    A. make critical appraisals of their work frequently
    B. encourage them to make suggestions
    C. make no change without their approval
    D. hold regular staff meetings

    23.____

24. A good relationship with other supervisors is important to a senior supervisor. Close cooperation among supervisory personnel is MOST likely to result in
    A. increasing the probability for support of supervisory actions and decisions
    B. stimulating supervisors to achieve higher status in the organization
    C. helping to control the flow of work within a unit
    D. a clearer definition of the responsibilities of individual supervisors

24._____

25. Which of the following is MOST likely to gain a supervisor the respect and cooperation of his staff?
    A. Assigning the most difficult jobs to the experienced staff members
    B. Giving each staff member the same number of assignments
    C. Assigning jobs according to each staff member's ability
    D. Giving each staff member the same types of assignments

25._____

KEY (CORRECT ANSWERS)

1.	D		11.	C
2.	A		12.	D
3.	D		13.	C
4.	B		14.	C
5.	D		15.	B
6.	B		16.	D
7.	A		17.	A
8.	D		18.	A
9.	D		19.	A
10.	C		20.	B

21. A
22. A
23. B
24. A
25. C

PHILOSOPHY, PRINCIPLES, PRACTICES, AND TECHNICS
OF
SUPERVISION, ADMINISTRATION, MANAGEMENT, AND ORGANIZATION

TABLE OF CONTENTS

	Page
MEANING OF SUPERVISION	1
THE OLD AND THE NEW SUPERVISION	1
THE EIGHT (8) BASIC PRINCIPLES OF THE NEW SUPERVISION	1
I. Principle of Responsibility	1
II. Principle of Authority	2
III. Principle of Self-Growth	2
IV. Principle of Individual Worth	2
V. Principle of Creative Leadership	2
VI. Principle of Success and Failure	2
VII. Principle of Science	3
VIII. Principle of Cooperation	3
WHAT IS ADMINISTRATION?	3
I. Practices Commonly Classed as "Supervisory"	3
II. Practices Commonly Classed as "Administrative"	3
III. Practices Commonly Classed as Both "Supervisory" and "Administrative"	4
RESPONSIBILITIES OF THE SUPERVISOR	4
COMPETENCIES OF THE SUPERVISOR	4
THE PROFESSIONAL SUPERVISOR-EMPLOYEE RELATIONSHIP	4
MINI-TEXT IN SUPERVISION, ADMINISTRATION, MANAGEMENT, AND ORGANIZATION	5
I. Brief Highlights	5
A. Levels of Management	6
B. What the Supervisor Must Learn	6
C. A Definition of Supervision	6
D. Elements of the Team Concept	6
E. Principles of Organization	6
F. The Four Important Parts of Every Job	7
G. Principles of Delegation	7
H. Principles of Effective Communications	7
I. Principles of Work Improvement	7
J. Areas of Job Improvement	7
K. Seven Key Points in Making Improvements	8

	L.	Corrective Techniques for Job Improvement	8
	M.	A Planning Checklist	8
	N.	Five Characteristics of Good Directions	9
	O.	Types of Directions	9
	P.	Controls	9
	Q.	Orienting the New Employee	9
	R.	Checklist for Orienting New Employees	9
	S.	Principles of Learning	10
	T.	Causes of Poor Performance	10
	U.	Four Major Steps in On-the-Job Instructions	10
	V.	Employees Want Five Things	10
	W.	Some Don'ts in Regard to Praise	11
	X.	How to Gain Your Workers' Confidence	11
	Y.	Sources of Employee Problems	11
	Z.	The Supervisor's Key to Discipline	11
	AA.	Five Important Processes of Management	12
	BB.	When the Supervisor Fails to Plan	12
	CC.	Fourteen General Principles of Management	12
	DD.	Change	12
II.	Brief Topical Summaries		13
	A.	Who/What is the Supervisor?	13
	B.	The Sociology of Work	13
	C.	Principles and Practices of Supervision	14
	D.	Dynamic Leadership	14
	E.	Processes for Solving Problems	15
	F.	Training for Results	15
	G.	Health, Safety, and Accident Prevention	16
	H.	Equal Employment Opportunity	16
	I.	Improving Communications	16
	J.	Self-Development	17
	K.	Teaching and Training	17
		1. The Teaching Process	17
		a. Preparation	17
		b. Presentation	18
		c. Summary	18
		d. Application	18
		e. Evaluation	18
		2. Teaching Methods	18
		a. Lecture	18
		b. Discussion	18
		c. Demonstration	19
		d. Performance	19
		e. Which Method to Use	19

PHILOSOPHY, PRINCIPLES, PRACTICES, AND TECHNICS
OF
SUPERVISION, ADMINISTRATION, MANAGEMENT, AND ORGANIZATION

MEANING OF SUPERVISION

The extension of the democratic philosophy has been accompanied by an extension in the scope of supervision. Modern leaders and supervisors no longer think of supervision in the narrow sense of being confined chiefly to visiting employees, supplying materials, or rating the staff. They regard supervision as being intimately related to all the concerned agencies of society, they speak of the supervisor's function in terms of "growth," rather than the "improvement" of employees.

This modern concept of supervision may be defined as follows: Supervision is leadership and the development of leadership within groups which are cooperatively engaged in inspection, research, training, guidance, and evaluation.

THE OLD AND THE NEW SUPERVISION

TRADITIONAL
1. Inspection
2. Focused on the employee
3. Visitation
4. Random and haphazard
5. Imposed and authoritarian
6. One person usually

MODERN
1. Study and analysis
2. Focused on aims, materials, methods, supervisors, employees, environment
3. Demonstrations, intervisitation, workshops, directed reading, bulletins, etc.
4. Definitely organized and planned (scientific)
5. Cooperative and democratic
6. Many persons involved (creative)

THE EIGHT (8) BASIC PRINCIPLES OF THE NEW SUPERVISION

I. Principle of Responsibility
   Authority to act and responsibility for acting must be joined.
   A. If you give responsibility, give authority.
   B. Define employee duties clearly.
   C. Protect employees from criticism by others.
   D. Recognize the rights as well as obligations of employees.
   E. Achieve the aims of a democratic society insofar as it is possible within the area of your work.
   F. Establish a situation favorable to training and learning.
   G. Accept ultimate responsibility for everything done in your section, unit, office, division, department.
   H. Good administration and good supervision are inseparable.

II. Principle of Authority
The success of the supervisor is measured by the extent to which the power of authority is not used.
   A. Exercise simplicity and informality in supervision
   B. Use the simplest machinery of supervision
   C. If it is good for the organization as a whole, it is probably justified.
   D. Seldom be arbitrary or authoritative.
   E. Do not base your work on the power of position or of personality.
   F. Permit and encourage the free expression of opinions.

III. Principle of Self-Growth
The success of the supervisor is measured by the extent to which, and the speed with which, he is no longer needed.
   A. Base criticism on principles, not on specifics.
   B. Point out higher activities to employees.
   C. Train for self-thinking by employees to meet new situations.
   D. Stimulate initiative, self-reliance, and individual responsibility
   E. Concentrate on stimulating the growth of employees rather than on removing defects.

IV. Principle of Individual Worth
Respect for the individual is a paramount consideration in supervision.
   A. Be human and sympathetic in dealing with employees.
   B. Don't nag about things to be done.
   C. Recognize the individual differences among employees and seek opportunities to permit best expression of each personality.

V. Principle of Creative Leadership
The best supervision is that which is not apparent to the employee.
   A. Stimulate, don't drive employees to creative action.
   B. Emphasize doing good things.
   C. Encourage employees to do what they do best.
   D. Do not be too greatly concerned with details of subject or method.
   E. Do not be concerned exclusively with immediate problems and activities.
   F. Reveal higher activities and make them both desired and maximally possible.
   G. Determine procedures in the light of each situation but see that these are derived from a sound basic philosophy.
   H. Aid, inspire, and lead so as to liberate the creative spirit latent in all good employees.

VI. Principle of Success and Failure
There are no unsuccessful employees, only unsuccessful supervisors who have failed to give proper leadership.
   A. Adapt suggestions to the capacities, attitudes, and prejudices of employees.
   B. Be gradual, be progressive, be persistent.
   C. Help the employee find the general principle; have the employee apply his own problem to the general principle.
   D. Give adequate appreciation for good work and honest effort.
   E. Anticipate employee difficulties and help to prevent them.
   F. Encourage employees to do the desirable things they will do anyway.
   G. Judge your supervision by the results it secures.

VII. Principle of Science
Successful supervision is scientific, objective, and experimental. It is based on facts, not on prejudices.
  A. Be cumulative in results.
  B. Never divorce your suggestions from the goals of training.
  C. Don't be impatient of results.
  D. Keep all matters on a professional, not a personal, level.
  E. Do not be concerned exclusively with immediate problems and activities.
  F. Use objective means of determining achievement and rating where possible.

VIII. Principle of Cooperation
Supervision is a cooperative enterprise between supervisor and employee.
  A. Begin with conditions as they are.
  B. Ask opinions of all involved when formulating policies.
  C. Organization is as good as its weakest link.
  D. Let employees help to determine policies and department programs.
  E. Be approachable and accessible—physically and mentally.
  F. Develop pleasant social relationships.

WHAT IS ADMINISTRATION

Administration is concerned with providing the environment, the material facilities, and the operational procedures that will promote the maximum growth and development of supervisors and employees. (Organization is an aspect and a concomitant of administration.)

There is no sharp line of demarcation between supervision and administration; these functions are intimately interrelated and, often, overlapping. They are complementary activities.

I. Practices Commonly Classed as "Supervisory"
  A. Conducting employees' conferences
  B. Visiting sections, units, offices, divisions, departments
  C. Arranging for demonstrations
  D. Examining plans
  E. Suggesting professional reading
  F. Interpreting bulletins
  G. Recommending in-service training courses
  H. Encouraging experimentation
  I. Appraising employee morale
  J. Providing for intervisitation

II. Practices Commonly Classified as "Administrative"
  A. Management of the office
  B. Arrangement of schedules for extra duties
  C. Assignment of rooms or areas
  D. Distribution of supplies
  E. Keeping records and reports
  F. Care of audio-visual materials
  G. Keeping inventory records
  H. Checking record cards and books

  I. Programming special activities
  J. Checking on the attendance and punctuality of employees

III. Practices Commonly Classified as Both "Supervisory" and "Administrative"
  A. Program construction
  B. Testing or evaluating outcomes
  C. Personnel accounting
  D. Ordering instructional materials

RESPONSIBILITIES OF THE SUPERVISOR

A person employed in a supervisory capacity must constantly be able to improve his own efficiency and ability. He represent the employer to the employees and only continuous self-examination can make him a capable supervisor.

Leadership and training are the supervisor's responsibility. An efficient working unit is one in which the employees work with the supervisor. It is his job to bring out the best in his employees. He must always be relaxed, courteous, and calm in his association with his employees. Their feelings are important, and a harsh attitude does not develop the most efficient employees.

COMPETENCES OF THE SUPERVISOR

  I. Complete knowledge of the duties and responsibilities of his position.
  II. To be able to organize a job, plan ahead, and carry through.
  III. To have self-confidence and initiative.
  IV. To be able to handle the unexpected situation and make quick decisions.
  V. To be able to properly train subordinates in the positions they are best suited for.
  VI. To be able to keep good human relations among his subordinates.
  VII. To be able to keep good human relations between his subordinates and himself and to earn their respect and trust.

THE PROFESSIONAL SUPERVISOR-EMPLOYEE RELATIONSHIP

There are two kinds of efficiency: one kind is only apparent and is produced in organizations through the exercise of mere discipline; this is but a simulation of the second, or true, efficiency which springs from spontaneous cooperation. If you are a manager, no matter how great or small your responsibility, it is your job, in the final analysis, to create and develop this involuntary cooperation among the people whom you supervise. For, no matter how powerful a combination of money, machines, and materials a company may have, this is a dead and sterile thing without a team of willing, thinking, and articulate people to guide it.

The following 21 points are presented as indicative of the exemplary basic relationship that should exist between supervisor and employee:

1. Each person wants to be liked and respected by his fellow employee and wants to be treated with consideration and respect by his superior.
2. The most competent employee will make an error. However, in a unit where good relations exist between the supervisor and his employees, tenseness and fear do not exist. Thus, errors are not hidden or covered up, and the efficiency of a unit is not impaired.

3. Subordinates resent rules, regulations, or orders that are unreasonable or unexplained.
4. Subordinates are quick to resent unfairness, harshness, injustices, and favoritism.
5. An employee will accept responsibility if he knows that he will be complimented for a job well done, and not too harshly chastised for failure; that his supervisor will check the cause of the failure, and, if it was the supervisor's fault, he will assume the blame therefore. If it was the employee's fault, his supervisor will explain the correct method or means of handling the responsibility.
6. An employee wants to receive credit for a suggestion he has made, that is used. If a suggestion cannot be used, the employee is entitled to an explanation. The supervisor should not say "no" and close the subject.
7. Fear and worry slow up a worker's ability. Poor working environment can impair his physical and mental health. A good supervisor avoids forceful methods, threats, and arguments to get a job done.
8. A forceful supervisor is able to train his employees individually and as a team, and is able to motivate them in the proper channels.
9. A mature supervisor is able to properly evaluate his subordinates and to keep them happy and satisfied.
10. A sensitive supervisor will never patronize his subordinates.
11. A worthy supervisor will respect his employees' confidences.
12. Definite and clear-cut responsibilities should be assigned to each executive.
13. Responsibility should always be coupled with corresponding authority.
14. No change should be made in the scope or responsibilities of a position without a definite understanding to that effect on the part of all persons concerned.
15. No executive or employee, occupying a single position in the organization, should be subject to definite orders from more than one source.
16. Orders should never be given to subordinates over the head of a responsible executive. Rather than do this, the officer in question should be supplanted.
17. Criticisms of subordinates should, whoever possible, be made privately, and in no case should a subordinate be criticized in the presence of executives or employees of equal or lower rank.
18. No dispute or difference between executives or employees as to authority or responsibilities should be considered too trivial for prompt and careful adjudication.
19. Promotions, wage changes, and disciplinary action should always be approved by the executive immediately superior to the one directly responsible.
20. No executive or employee should ever be required, or expected, to be at the same time an assistant to, and critic of, another.
21. Any executive whose work is subject to regular inspection should, wherever practicable, be given the assistance and facilities necessary to enable him to maintain an independent check of the quality of his work.

MINI-TEXT IN SUPERVISION, ADMINISTRATION, MANAGEMENT, AND ORGANIZATION

I. Brief Highlights

Listed concisely and sequentially are major headings and important data in the field for quick recall and review.

A. Levels of Management
    Any organization of some size has several levels of management. In terms of a ladder, the levels are:

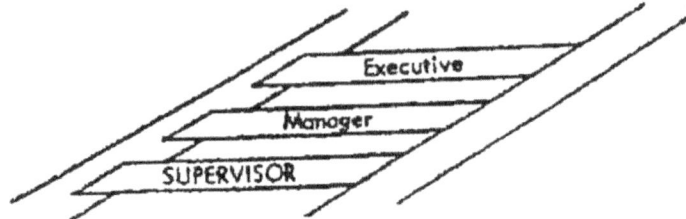

The first level is very important because it is the beginning point of management leadership.

B. What the Supervisor Must Learn
    A supervisor must learn to:
    1. Deal with people and their differences
    2. Get the job done through people
    3. Recognize the problems when they exist
    4. Overcome obstacles to good performance
    5. Evaluate the performance of people
    6. Check his own performance in terms of accomplishment

C. A Definition of Supervisor
    The term supervisor means any individual having authority, in the interests of the employer, to hire, transfer, suspend, lay-off, recall, promote, discharge, assign, reward, or discipline other employees or responsibility to direct them, or to adjust their grievances, or effectively to recommend such action, if, in connection with the foregoing, exercise of such authority is not of a merely routine or clerical nature but requires the use of independent judgment.

D. Elements of the Team Concept
    What is involved in teamwork? The component parts are:
    1. Members
    2. A leader
    3. Goals
    4. Plans
    5. Cooperation
    6. Spirit

E. Principles of Organization
    1. A team member must know what his job is.
    2. Be sure that the nature and scope of a job are understood.
    3. Authority and responsibility should be carefully spelled out.
    4. A supervisor should be permitted to make the maximum number of decisions affecting his employees.
    5. Employees should report to only one supervisor.
    6. A supervisor should direct only as many employees as he can handle effectively.
    7. An organization plan should be flexible.

8. Inspection and performance of work should be separate.
9. Organizational problems should receive immediate attention.
10. Assign work in line with ability and experience.

F. The Four Important Parts of Every Job
1. Inherent in every job is the *accountability* for results.
2. A second set of factors in every job is *responsibilities*.
3. Along with duties and responsibilities one must have the *authority* to act within certain limits without obtaining permission to proceed.
4. No job exists in a vacuum. The supervisor is surrounded by key *relationships*.

G. Principles of Delegation
Where work is delegated for the first time, the supervisor should think in terms of these questions:
1. Who is best qualified to do this?
2. Can an employee improve his abilities by doing this?
3. How long should an employee spend on this?
4. Are there any special problems for which he will need guidance?
5. How broad a delegation can I make?

H. Principles of Effective Communications
1. Determine the media.
2. To whom directed?
3. Identification and source authority.
4. Is communication understood?

I. Principles of Work Improvement
1. Most people usually do only the work which is assigned to them.
2. Workers are likely to fit assigned work into the time available to perform it.
3. A good workload usually stimulates output.
4. People usually do their best work when they know that results will be reviewed or inspected.
5. Employees usually feel that someone else is responsible for conditions of work, workplace layout, job methods, type of tools/equipment, and other such factors.
6. Employees are usually defensive about their job security.
7. Employees have natural resistance to change.
8. Employees can support or destroy a supervisor.
9. A supervisor usually earns the respect of his people through his personal example of diligence and efficiency.

J. Areas of Job Improvement
The areas of job improvement are quite numerous, but the most common ones which a supervisor can identify and utilize are:
1. Departmental layout
2. Flow of work
3. Workplace layout
4. Utilization of manpower
5. Work methods
6. Materials handling

7. Utilization
8. Motion economy

K. Seven Key Points in Making Improvements
1. Select the job to be improved
2. Study how it is being done now
3. Question the present method
4. Determine actions to be taken
5. Chart proposed method
6. Get approval and apply
7. Solicit worker participation

l. Corrective Techniques of Job Improvement
Specific Problems
1. Size of workload
2. Inability to meet schedules
3. Strain and fatigue
4. Improper use of men and skills
5. Waste, poor quality, unsafe conditions
6. Bottleneck conditions that hinder output
7. Poor utilization of equipment and machine
8. Efficiency and productivity of labor

General Improvement
1. Departmental layout
2. Flow of work
3. Work plan layout
4. Utilization of manpower
5. Work methods
6. Materials handling
7. Utilization of equipment
8. Motion economy

Corrective Techniques
1. Study with scale model
2. Flow chart study
3. Motion analysis
4. Comparison of units produced to standard allowance
5. Methods analysis
6. Flow chart and equipment study
7. Down time vs. running time
8. Motion analysis

M. A Planning Checklist
1. Objectives
2. Controls
3. Delegations
4. Communications
5. Resources
6. Manpower

7. Equipment
8. Supplies and materials
9. Utilization of time
10. Safety
11. Money
12. Work
13. Timing of improvements

N. Five Characteristics of Good Directions
In order to get results, directions must be:
1. Possible of accomplishment
2. Agreeable with worker interests
3. Related to mission
4. Planned and complete
5. Unmistakably clear

O. Types of Directions
1. Demands or direct orders
2. Requests
3. Suggestion or implication
4. volunteering

P. Controls
A typical listing of the overall areas in which the supervisor should establish controls might be:
1. Manpower
2. Materials
3. Quality of work
4. Quantity of work
5. Time
6. Space
7. Money
8. Methods

Q. Orienting the New Employee
1. Prepare for him
2. Welcome the new employee
3. Orientation for the job
4. Follow-up

R. Checklist for Orienting New Employees   Yes   No
1. Do you appreciate the feelings of new employees
   when they first report for work?   ___   ___
2. Are you aware of the fact that the new employee must
   make a big adjustment to his job?   ___   ___
3. Have you given him good reasons for liking the job and
   the organization?   ___   ___
4. Have you prepared for his first day on the job?   ___   ___
5. Did you welcome him cordially and make him feel needed?   ___   ___

	Yes	No

6. Did you establish rapport with him so that he feels free to talk and discuss matters with you? ___ ___
7. Did you explain his job to him and his relationship to you? ___ ___
8. Does he know that his work will be evaluated periodically on a basis that is fair and objective? ___ ___
9. Did you introduce him to his fellow workers in such a way that they are likely to accept him? ___ ___
10. Does he know what employee benefits he will receive? ___ ___
11. Does he understand the importance of being on the job and what to do if he must leave his duty station? ___ ___
12. Has he been impressed with the importance of accident prevention and safe practice? ___ ___
13. Does he generally know his way around the department? ___ ___
14. Is he under the guidance of a sponsor who will teach the right way of doing things? ___ ___
15. Do you plan to follow-up so that he will continue to adjust successfully to his job? ___ ___

S. Principles of Learning
   1. Motivation
   2. Demonstration or explanation
   3. Practice

T. Causes of Poor Performance
   1. Improper training for job
   2. Wrong tools
   3. Inadequate directions
   4. Lack of supervisory follow-up
   5. Poor communications
   6. Lack of standards of performance
   7. Wrong work habits
   8. Low morale
   9. Other

U. Four Major Steps in On-The-Job Instruction
   1. Prepare the worker
   2. Present the operation
   3. Tryout performance
   4. Follow-up

V. Employees Want Five Things
   1. Security
   2. Opportunity
   3. Recognition
   4. Inclusion
   5. Expression

W. Some Don'ts in Regard to Praise
1. Don't praise a person for something he hasn't done.
2. Don't praise a person unless you can be sincere.
3. Don't be sparing in praise just because your superior withholds it from you.
4. Don't let too much time elapse between good performance and recognition of it

X. How to Gain Your Workers' Confidence
Methods of developing confidence include such things as:
1. Knowing the interests, habits, hobbies of employees
2. Admitting your own inadequacies
3. Sharing and telling of confidence in others
4. Supporting people when they are in trouble
5. Delegating matters that can be well handled
6. Being frank and straightforward about problems and working conditions
7. Encouraging others to bring their problems to you
8. Taking action on problems which impede worker progress

Y. Sources of Employee Problems
On-the-job causes might be such things as:
1. A feeling that favoritism is exercised in assignments
2. Assignment of overtime
3. An undue amount of supervision
4. Changing methods or systems
5. Stealing of ideas or trade secrets
6. Lack of interest in job
7. Threat of reduction in force
8. Ignorance or lack of communications
9. Poor equipment
10. Lack of knowing how supervisor feels toward employee
11. Shift assignments

Off-the-job problems might have to do with:
1. Health
2. Finances
3. Housing
4. Family

Z. The Supervisor's Key to Discipline
There are several key points about discipline which the supervisor should keep in mind:
1. Job discipline is one of the disciplines of life and is directed by the supervisor.
2. It is more important to correct an employee fault than to fix blame for it.
3. Employee performance is affected by problems both on the job and off.
4. Sudden or abrupt changes in behavior can be indications of important employee problems.
5. Problems should be dealt with as soon as possible after they are identified.
6. The attitude of the supervisor may have more to do with solving problems than the techniques of problem solving.
7. Correction of employee behavior should be resorted to only after the supervisor is sure that training or counseling will not be helpful.

8. Be sure to document your disciplinary actions.
9. Make sure that you are disciplining on the basis of facts rather than personal feelings.
10. Take each disciplinary step in order, being careful not to make snap judgments, or decisions based on impatience.

AA. Five Important Processes of Management
1. Planning
2. Organizing
3. Scheduling
4. Controlling
5. Motivating

BB. When the Supervisor Fails to Plan
1. Supervisor creates impression of not knowing his job
2. May lead to excessive overtime
3. Job runs itself—supervisor lacks control
4. Deadlines and appointments missed
5. Parts of the work go undone
6. Work interrupted by emergencies
7. Sets a bad example
8. Uneven workload creates peaks and valleys
9. Too much time on minor details at expense of more important tasks

CC. Fourteen General Principles of Management
1. Division of work
2. Authority and responsibility
3. Discipline
4. Unity of command
5. Unity of direction
6. Subordination of individual interest to general interest
7. Remuneration of personnel
8. Centralization
9. Scalar chain
10. Order
11. Equity
12. Stability of tenure of personnel
13. Initiative
14. Esprit de corps

DD. Change

Bringing about change is perhaps attempted more often, and yet less well understood, than anything else the supervisor does. How do people generally react to change? (People tend to resist change that is imposed upon them by other individuals or circumstances.

Change is characteristic of every situation. It is a part of every real endeavor where the efforts of people are concerned.

1. Why do people resist change?
   People may resist change because of:
   a. Fear of the unknown
   b. Implied criticism
   c. Unpleasant experiences in the past
   d. Fear of loss of status
   e. Threat to the ego
   f. Fear of loss of economic stability

2. How can we best overcome the resistance to change?
   In initiating change, take these steps:
   a. Get ready to sell
   b. Identify sources of help
   c. Anticipate objections
   d. Sell benefits
   e. Listen in depth
   f. Follow up

II. Brief Topical Summaries

   A. Who/What is the Supervisor?
      1. The supervisor is often called the "highest level employee and the lowest level manager."
      2. A supervisor is a member of both management and the work group. He acts as a bridge between the two.
      3. Most problems in supervision are in the area of human relations, or people problems.
      4. Employees expect: Respect, opportunity to learn and to advance, and a sense of belonging, and so forth.
      5. Supervisors are responsible for directing people and organizing work. Planning is of paramount importance.
      6. A position description is a set of duties and responsibilities inherent to a given position.
      7. It is important to keep the position description up-to-date and to provide each employee with his own copy.

   B. The Sociology of Work
      1. People are alike in many ways; however, each individual is unique.
      2. The supervisor is challenged in getting to know employee differences. Acquiring skills in evaluating individuals is an asset.
      3. Maintaining meaningful working relationships in the organization is of great importance.
      4. The supervisor has an obligation to help individuals to develop to their fullest potential.
      5. Job rotation on a planned basis helps to build versatility and to maintain interest and enthusiasm in work groups.
      6. Cross training (job rotation) provides backup skills.

7. The supervisor can help reduce tension by maintaining a sense of humor, providing guidance to employees, and by making reasonable and timely decisions. Employees respond favorably to working under reasonably predictable circumstances.
8. Change is characteristic of all managerial behavior. The supervisor must adjust to changes in procedures, new methods, technological changes, and to a number of new and sometimes challenging situations.
9. To overcome the natural tendency for people to resist change, the supervisor should become more skillful in initiating change.

C. Principles and Practices of Supervision
1. Employees should be required to answer to only one superior.
2. A supervisor can effectively direct only a limited number of employees, depending upon the complexity, variety, and proximity of the jobs involved.
3. The organizational chart presents the organization in graphic form. It reflects lines of authority and responsibility as well as interrelationships of units within the organization.
4. Distribution of work can be improved through an analysis using the "Work Distribution Chart."
5. The "Work Distribution Chart" reflects the division of work within a unit in understandable form.
6. When related tasks are given to an employee, he has a better chance of increasing his skills through training.
7. The individual who is given the responsibility for tasks must also be given the appropriate authority to insure adequate results.
8. The supervisor should delegate repetitive, routine work. Preparation of recurring reports, maintaining leave and attendance records are some examples.
9. Good discipline is essential to good task performance. Discipline is reflected in the actions of employees on the job in the absence of supervision.
10. Disciplinary action may have to be taken when the positive aspects of discipline have failed. Reprimand, warning, and suspension are examples of disciplinary action.
11. If a situation calls for a reprimand, be sure it is deserved and remember it is to be done in private.

D. Dynamic Leadership
1. A style is a personal method or manner of exerting influence.
2. Authoritarian leaders often see themselves as the source of power and authority.
3. The democratic leader often perceives the group as the source of authority and power.
4. Supervisors tend to do better when using the pattern of leadership that is most natural for them.
5. Social scientists suggest that the effective supervisor use the leadership style that best fits the problem or circumstances involved.
6. All four styles—telling, selling, consulting, joining—have their place. Using one does not preclude using the other at another time.

7. The theory X point of view assumes that the average person dislikes work, will avoid it whenever possible, and must be coerced to achieve organizational objectives.
8. The theory Y point of view assumes that the average person considers work to be a natural as play, and, when the individual is committed, he requires little supervision or direction to accomplish desired objectives.
9. The leader's basic assumptions concerning human behavior and human nature affect his actions, decisions, and other managerial practices.
10. Dissatisfaction among employees is often present, but difficult to isolate. The supervisor should seek to weaken dissatisfaction by keeping promises, being sincere and considerate, keeping employees informed, and so forth.
11. Constructive suggestions should be encouraged during the natural progress of the work.

E. Processes for Solving Problems
1. People find their daily tasks more meaningful and satisfying when they can improve them.
2. The causes of problems, or the key factors, are often hidden in the background. Ability to solve problems often involves the ability to isolate them from their backgrounds. There is some substance to the cliché that some persons "can't see the forest for the trees."
3. New procedures are often developed from old ones. Problems should be broken down into manageable parts. New ideas can be adapted from old one.
4. People think differently in problem-solving situations. Using a logical, patterned approach is often useful. One approach found to be useful includes these steps:
   a. Define the problem
   b. Establish objectives
   c. Get the facts
   d. Weigh and decide
   e. Take action
   f. Evaluate action

F. Training for Results
1. Participants respond best when they feel training is important to them.
2. The supervisor has responsibility for the training and development of those who report to him.
3. When training is delegated to others, great care must be exercised to insure the trainer has knowledge, aptitude, and interest for his work as a trainer.
4. Training (learning) of some type goes on continually. The most successful supervisor makes certain the learning contributes in a productive manner to operational goals.
5. New employees are particularly susceptible to training. Older employees facing new job situations require specific training, as well as having need for development and growth opportunities.
6. Training needs require continuous monitoring.
7. The training officer of an agency is a professional with a responsibility to assist supervisors in solving training problems.

8. Many of the self-development steps important to the supervisor's own growth are equally important to the development of peers and subordinates. Knowledge of these is important when the supervisor consults with others on development and growth opportunities.

G. Health, Safety, and Accident Prevention
1. Management-minded supervisors take appropriate measures to assist employees in maintaining health and in assuring safe practices in the work environment.
2. Effective safety training and practices help to avoid injury and accidents.
3. Safety should be a management goal. All infractions of safety which are observed should be corrected without exception.
4. Employees' safety attitude, training and instruction, provision of safe tools and equipment, supervision, and leadership are considered highly important factors which contribute to safety and which can be influenced directly by supervisors.
5. When accidents do occur, they should be investigated promptly for very important reasons, including the fact that information which is gained can be used to prevent accidents in the future.

H. Equal Employment Opportunity
1. The supervisor should endeavor to treat all employees fairly, without regard to religion, race, sex, or national origin.
2. Groups tend to reflect the attitude of the leader. Prejudice can be detected even in very subtle form. Supervisors must strive to create a feeling of mutual respect and confidence in every employee.
3. Complete utilization of all human resources is a national goal. Equitable consideration should be accorded women in the work force, minority-group members, the physically and mentally handicapped, and the older employee. The important question is: "Who can do the job?"
4. Training opportunities, recognition for performance, overtime assignments, promotional opportunities, and all other personnel actions are to be handled on an equitable basis.

I. Improving Communications
1. Communications is achieving understanding between the sender and the receiver of a message. It also means sharing information—the creation of understanding.
2. Communication is basic to all human activity. Words are means of conveying meanings; however, real meanings are in people.
3. There are very practical differences in the effectiveness of one-way, impersonal, and two-way communications. Words spoken face-to-face are better understood. Telephone conversations are effective, but lack the rapport of person-to-person exchanges. The whole person communicates.
4. Cooperation and communication in an organization go hand in hand. When there is a mutual respect between people, spelling out rules and procedures for communicating is unnecessary.
5. There are several barriers to effective communications. These include failure to listen with respect and understanding, lack of skill in feedback, and misinterpreting the meanings of words used by the speaker. It is also common

practice to listen to what we want to hear, and tune out things we do not want to hear.
6. Communication is management's chief problem. The supervisor should accept the challenge to communicate more effectively and to improve interagency and intra-agency communications.
7. The supervisor may often plan for and conduct meetings. The planning phase is critical and may determine the success or the failure of a meeting.
8. Speaking before groups usually requires extra effort. Stage fright may never disappear completely, but it can be controlled.

J. Self-Development
1. Every employee is responsible for his own self-development.
2. Toastmaster and toastmistress clubs offer opportunities to improve skills in oral communications.
3. Planning for one's own self-development is of vital importance. Supervisors know their own strengths and limitations better than anyone else.
4. Many opportunities are open to aid the supervisor in his developmental efforts, including job assignments; training opportunities, both governmental and non-governmental—to include universities and professional conferences and seminars.
5. Programmed instruction offers a means of studying at one's own rate.
6. Where difficulties may arise from a supervisor's being away from his work for training, he may participate in televised home study or correspondence courses to meet his self-development needs.

K. Teaching and Training
1. The Teaching Process
Teaching is encouraging and guiding the learning activities of students toward established goals. In most cases this process consists of five steps: preparation, presentation, summarization, evaluation, and application.

   a. Preparation
   Preparation is two-fold in nature; that of the supervisor and the employee. Preparation by the supervisor is absolutely essential to success. He must know what, when, where, how, and whom he will teach. Some of the factors that should be considered are:
   1) The objectives
   2) The materials needed
   3) The methods to be used
   4) Employee participation
   5) Employee interest
   6) Training aids
   7) Evaluation
   8) Summarization

   Employee preparation consists in preparing the employee to receive the material. Probably the most important single factor in the preparation of the employee is arousing and maintaining his interest. He must know the objectives of the training, why he is there, how the material can be used, and its importance to him.

b. Presentation
In presentation, have a carefully designed plan and follow it. The plan should be accurate and complete, yet flexible enough to meet situations as they arise. The method of presentation will be determined by the particular situation and objectives.

c. Summary
A summary should be made at the end of every training unit and program. In addition, there may be internal summaries depending on the nature of the material being taught. The important thing is that the trainee must always be able to understand how each part of the new material relates to the whole.

d. Application
The supervisor must arrange work so the employee will be given a chance to apply new knowledge or skills while the material is still clear in his mind and interest is high. The trainee does not really know whether he has learned the material until he has been given a chance to apply it. If the material is not applied, it loses most of its value.

e. Evaluation
The purpose of all training is to promote learning. To determine whether the training has been a success or failure, the supervisor must evaluate this learning.
In the broadest sense, evaluation includes all the devices, methods, skills, and techniques used by the supervisor to keep himself and the employees informed as to their progress toward the objectives they are pursuing. The extent to which the employee has mastered the knowledge, skills, and abilities, or changed his attitudes, as determined by the program objectives, is the extent to which instruction has succeeded or failed.
Evaluation should not be confined to the end of the lesson, day, or program but should be used continuously. We shall note later the way this relates to the rest of the teaching process.

2. Teaching Methods
A teaching method is a pattern of identifiable student and instructor activity used in presenting training material.
All supervisors are faced with the problem of deciding which method should be used at a given time.

a. Lecture
The lecture is direct oral presentation of material by the supervisor. The present trend is to place less emphasis on the trainer's activity and more on that of the trainee.

b. Discussion
Teaching by discussion or conference involves using questions and other techniques to arouse interest and focus attention upon certain areas, and by doing so creating a learning situation. This can be one of the most

valuable methods because it gives the employees an opportunity to express their ideas and pool their knowledge.

    c. Demonstration
The demonstration is used to teach how something works or how to do something. It can be used to show a principle or what the results of a series of actions will be. A well-staged demonstration is particularly effective because it shows proper methods of performance in a realistic manner.

    d. Performance
Performance is one of the most fundamental of all learning techniques or teaching methods. The trainee may be able to tell how a specific operation should be performed but he cannot be sure he knows how to perform the operation until he has done so.
As with all methods, there are certain advantages and disadvantages to each method.

    e. Which Method to Use
Moreover, there are other methods and techniques of teaching. It is difficult to use any method without other methods entering into it. In any learning situation, a combination of methods is usually more effective than any one method alone.

Finally, evaluation must be integrated into the other aspects of the teaching-learning process.

It must be used in the motivation of the trainees; it must be used to assist in developing understanding during the training; and it must be related to employee application of the results of training.

This is distinctly the role of the supervisor.

THE USE AND CARE OF TOOLS

CONTENTS

I. INTRODUCTION.
    1. Definitions
    2. Safety Precautions.

II. MEASURING TOOLS
    1. General
    2. Standards of Measurement
        a. Standards of Length
        b. Standards of Screw Threads
        c. Standards of Wire and Sheet Metal
        d. Standards of Weight
    3. Useful Measuring Tools
        a. Levels
        b. Plumb Bobs
        c. Scrivers
        d. Rules or Scales
        e. Precision Tapes
        f. Squares
        g. Calipers and Dividers h. Micrometers
        i. Surface, Depth, and Height Gages
        j. Plug, Ring, and Snap Gages and Gage Blocks
        k. Miscellaneous Measuring Gages

III. NONEDGED TOOLS
    1. General
    2. Useful Nonedged Tools
        a. Hammers and Mallets
        b. Screwdrivers
        c. Wrenches
        d. Pliers and Tongs
        e. Clamping Devices
        f. Jacks
        g. Bars and Mattock
        h. Soldering Irons
        i. Grinders and Sharpening Stones
        j. Benders and Pulters
        k. Torchers
        l. Blacksmith's Anvils and Iron Working Tools
        m. Breast Drill and Ratchet Bit Brace
        n. Sheet Metal Tools

IV. EDGED HANDTOOLS
    1. General
    2. Useful Edged Handtools
        a Chisels
        b. Files
        c. Knives

d. Scrapers
e. Punches
f. Awls
g. Shears, Nippers, and Pincers
h. Bolt, Cable, and Glass Cutters
i. Pipe and Tube Cutters, and Flaring Tools
j. Reamers
k. Taps and Dies
l. Thread Chasers
m. Screw and Tap Extractors

THE USE AND CARE OF TOOLS

I. INTRODUCTION

1. Definitions

    a. Handtools are defined as hand powered and hand operated tools that are designed to perform mechanical operations.
    b. Measuring tools are defined as tools that will measure work. Measuring tools can be classed as precision and non-precision tools.

2. Safety Precautions

    It is extremely important for all concerned to recognize the possibilities of injury when using handtools and measuring tools.
    The following safety precautions are included as a guide to prevent or minimize personal injury:

    a. Make certain all tool handles are securely attached before using them.
    b. Exercise extreme caution when handling edged tools.
    c. Do not use a tool for a purpose other than that for which it was intended.
    d. Do not handle tools carelessly carelessly piling tools in drawers, dropping tools on hard surfaces, etc., can damage tools. Damaged tools can cause mishaps.
    e. Keep your mind on your work so that you do not strike yourself or someone else with a hammer or sledge.
    f. Do not carry edged or pointed tools in your pocket.
    g. Always wear goggles when chipping metal and when grinding edges on tools.
    h. Hold driving tools correctly so that they will not slip off the work surface.
    i. Use the right tool for the job. The wrong tool may damage materials, injure workers, or both,
    j. Do not use punches with improper points or mushroomed heads,
    k. Do not use a tool that is oily or greasy. It may slip out of your hand, causing injury.
    l. When using jacks, make certain to use blocking or other supports when lifting a vehicle, in case of jack failure.
    m. Make sure work to be cut, sheared, chiseled, filed, etc., is steadied and secure, to prevent the tool from slipping.
    n. When using a knife, always cut away from your body, except in the case of a spoke shave or draw knife.
    o. Use torches and soldering irons with extreme care to prevent burns and explosions. The soldering iron must be so placed that the hot point cannot come in contact with flammable material or with the body.
    p. Familiarize yourself with the composition and hardness of the material to be worked.

II. MEASURING TOOLS
1. General

Measuring tools are designed for measuring work accurately. They include level indicating devices (levels), noncalibrated measuring tools (calipers, dividers, trammels) for transferring dimensions and/or layouts from one medium to another, calibrated measuring tools (rules, precision tapes, micrometers) designed to measure distances in accordance with one of several standards of measurement, gages (go and no-go gages, thread gages) which are machined to pre-determined shapes and/or sizes for measurement by comparison, and combination tools such as a combination square which is designed to perform two or more types of operation.

2. Standards of Measurement
    a. Standards of Length

    Two systems, the English and Metric, are commonly used in the design of measuring tools for linear measurements. The English system uses inches, feet, and yards, while the Metric system uses millimeters, centimeters, and meters. In relation to each other, 1 inch is equivalent to 25.4 millimeters, or 1 millimeter is equivalent to 0.039370 inch.

    b. Standards of Screw Threads

    There are several screw thread systems that are recognized as standards throughout the world. All threaded items for Ordnance use in the United States, Great Britain, and Canada are specified in the Unified System. The existing inch-measure screw-thread systems should be understood despite the existence of the Unified System.

(1) Inch-measure systems
    (a) Whitworth

    Introduced in England in 1941. The thread form is based on a 55 thread angle, and the crests and roots are rounded.

    (b) American National

    The American National screw-thread system was developed in 1933. This system is based on the 60 thread angle and the flat crests and roots and is included in the following series:
    1. Coarse thread sizes of 1 to 12 and 1/4 to 4".
    2. The fine thread series in sizes 0 to 12 and 1/4 to 1 1/2".
    3. The extra-fine thread series in sizes 0 to 12 and 1/2 to 2".
    4. The 8-pitch series in sizes from 1 to 6".
    5. The 12-pitch series from 1/2 to 6".
    6. The 16-pitch series from 3/4 to 4".

    (c) Classes of fit

    The American National screw-thread system calls for four regular classes of fit.

    Class 1. - Loose fit, with no possibility for interference between screw and tapped hole.

2. - Medium or free fit, but permitting slight interference in the worst combination of maximum screw and maximum nut.
3. - Close tolerances on mating parts may require this fit, applied to the highest grade of interchangeable work.
4. - A fine snug fit, where a screwdriver or wrench may be necessary for assembly.

NOTE: An additional Class 5, or jaw fit, is recognized for studs.

(2) Unified system

Since the whitworth and American National thread forms do not assemble because of the difference in thread angle, the 60 thread angle was adapted in 1949; however, the British may still use rounded crests and roots and their products will assemble with those made in United States plants. In the Unified system, class signifies tolerance, or tolerance and allowance. It is determined by the selected combination of classes for mating external and internal threads. New classes of tolerance are listed below: 3 for screws, 1A, 2A, and 3A; and 3 for nuts, IB, 2B, and 3B.

(a) Classes 1A and 1B, loose fit

A fit giving quick and easy assembly, even when threads are bruised or dirty. Applications: Ordnance and special uses.

(b) Classes 2A and 2B, medium fit

This fit permits wrenching with minimum galling and seizure. This medium fit is suited for the majority of commercial fasteners and is interchangeable with the American National Class 2 fit.

(c) Classes 3A and 3B, close fit

No allowance is provided. Applications are those where close fit and accuracy of lead and thread angle are required.

c. Standards of Wire and Sheet Metal

Sheet metal, strip, wire, and tubing are produced with thickness diameters or wall thicknesses, according to several gaging systems, depending on the article and metal. This situation is the result of natural development and preferences of the industries that produce these products. No single standard for all manufacturers has been established, since practical considerations stand in the way of adoption. In the case of steel, large users are thoroughly familiar with the behavior of existing gages in tooling, especially dies, and do not intend that their shop personnel be burdened with learning how preferred thicknesses behave. Another important factor is the sum total of orders of warehouse stock manufactured with existing gages. You must keep abreast of any change in availability of metals in these common gaging systems, as opposed to simplified systems.

For example; in the brass industry, the American Standards Association (ASA) numbers are said to be preferred for simplicity of stocking, but actually most of the metal is still made to Brown and Sharpe (B&S) gage numbers.

(1) Sheet metal gaging systems

Several gaging systems are used for sheet and strip metal.

  (a) Manufacturer's standard gaging system (Mfr's std)

  This gaging system is currently used for carbon and alloy sheets. This system is based on steel weighing 41.82 psf, 1 inch thick. Gage thickness equivalents are based on 0.0014945 in. per oz. per sq. ft.; 0.023912 in. per lb. per sq. ft. (reciprocal of 41.82 lb. per sq. ft. per in. thick); 3.443329 in. per lb. per sq. in.

  (b) U.S. standard gaging system (U.S. std)

  This gaging system is obsolete except for stainless steel sheets, cold-rolled steel strip (both carbon and alloy), stainless steel tubing, and nickel-alloy sheet and strip.

  (c) Birmingham wire gaging system (BWG)

  This gaging system is also called the Stubs iron wire gaging system, and is used for hot-rolled steel carbon and alloy strip and steel tubing.

  (d) Brown and Sharpe, or American wire gaging system (B&S or AWG)

  This gaging system is used for copper strip, brass and bronze sheet and strip, and aluminum and wire magnesium sheet.

(2) Wire gaging systems

  (a) Steel wire gaging system (SWG) or washburn & Moen gaging system

  This gaging system is used for steel wire, carbon steel mechanical spring wire, alloy-steel spring wire, stainless steel wire, and so forth. Carbon steel or music wire (wire used in the manufacture of musical instruments) is nominally specified to the sizes in the American Steel & Wire Company music wire sizes, although it is referred to by a number of other names found in steel catalogs.

  (b) Brown & Sharpe (B&S) or American wire gaging system (AWG)

  This gaging system is used for copper, copper alloy, aluminum, magnesium, nickel alloy, and other nonferrous metal wires used commercially.

(3) Rod gaging systems

  The Brown & Sharpe gaging system is used for copper, brass, and aluminum rods. Steel rods are nominally listed in fractional sizes, but drill rod may be listed in stubs steel wire gage or the twist drill and steel wire gage. It is preferable to refer to twist drill sizes in inch equivalents instead of the Stubs or twist drill numbers.

d. Standards of Weight

  Two standards of weight that are most commonly used are the Metric and English weight measures.

  (1) Metric standards

  The principal unit of weight in the Metric system is the gram (gm). Multiples of grams are obtained by prefixing the Greek words deka (10), hekto (100), and kilo (1,000). Divisions are obtained by prefixing the Latin words deci (1/10), centi (1/100), and milli (1/1000). The gram is the weight of 1 cubic centimeter of puje distilled water at a temperature of 39.2° F.; the kilogram is the weight of 1 liter (one cubic decimeter) of pureQdistilled water at a temperature of 39.2° F.; the metric ton is the weight of 1 cubic meter of pyre distilled water at a temperature of 39.2° F.

(2) English standards

The principal unit of weight in the English system is the grain (gr). We are more familiar with the ounce (oz), which is equal to 437.5 grains.

3. Useful Measuring Tools
   a. Levels
      (1) Purpose
         Levels are tools designed to prove whether a plane or surface is true horizontal or true vertical. Some levels are calibrated so that they will indicate the angle inclination in relation to a horizontal or vertical surface in degrees, minutes, and seconds.
   b. Plumb Bobs
      (1) Purpose
         The common plumb bob is used to determine true verticality. It is used in carpentry when erecting vertical uprights and corner posts of framework. Surveyors use it for transferring and lining up points. Special plumb bobs are designed for use with steel tapes or line to measure tank contents (oil, water, etc.).
   c. Scribers
      (1) Purpose
         Scribers are used to mark and lay out a pattern of work, to be followed in subsequent machining operations. Scribers are made for scribing, scoring, or marking many different materials such as glass, steel, aluminium, copper, and so forth.
   d. Rules or Scales
      (1) Purpose
         All rules (scales) are used to measure linear dimensions. They are read by a comparison of the etched lines on the scale with an edge or surface. Most scale dimensions are read with the naked eye, although a magnifying glass can be used to read graduations on a scale smaller than 1/64 inch.
   e. Precision Tapes
      (1) Purpose
         Precision tapes are used for measuring circumferences and long distances where rules cannot be applied.
   f. Squares
      (1) Purpose
         The purpose of a square is to test work for squareness and trueness. It is also used as a guide when marking work for subsequent machining, sawing, planing, and chiseling operations.
   g. Calipers and Dividers

(1) Purpose

Dividers are used for measuring distances between two points, for transferring or comparing measurements directly from a rule, or for scribing an arc, radius, or circle. Calipers are used for measuring diameters and distances, or for comparing dimensions or sizes with standards such as a graduated rule,

h. Micrometers

(1) Purpose

Micrometers are used for measurements requiring precise accuracy. They are more reliable and more accurate than the calipers listed in the preceding section.

i. Surface, Depth, and Height Gages

(1) Purpose

(a) Surface Gage

A surface gage is a measuring tool generally used to transfer measurements to work by scribing a line, and to indicate the accuracy or parallelism of surfaces.

(b) Depth Gage

A depth gage is an instrument adapted to measuring the depth of holes, slots, counterborers, recesses, and the distance from a surface to some recessed part.

(c) Height Gage

A height gage is used in the layout of jigs and fixtures, and on a bench, where it is used to check the location of holes and surfaces. It accurately measures and marks off vertical distances from a plane surface.

(d) Surface Plate

A surface plate provides a true, smooth, plane surface. It is often used in conjunction with surface and height gages as a level base on which the gages and parts are placed to obtain accurate measurements,

j. Plug, Ring, and Snap Gages and Gage Blocks

(1) Purpose

Plug, ring, and snap gages, and precision gage blocks are used as standards to determine whether or not one or more dimensions of a manufactured part are within specified limits. Their measurements are included in the construction of each gage, and they are called fixed gages; however, some snap gages are adjustable. In the average shop, gages are used for a wide range of work, from rough machining to the finest tool and die making. The accuracy required of the same type gage will be different, depending on the application. The following classes of gages and their limits of accuracy are standard for all makes:

Class XX(Male gages only).

Precision lapped to laboratory tolerances. For master or setup standards.

Class X

Precision lapped to close tolerances for many types of masters and the highest quality working and inspection gages.

Class Y

Good lapped finish to slightly increased tolerances for inspection and working gages.

Class Z

Commercial finish (ground and polished, but not fully lapped) for a large percentage of working gages in which tolerances are fairly wide, and where production quantities are not so large.

Class ZZ (Ring gages only)

Ground only to meet the demand for an inexpensive gage, where quantities are small and tolerances liberal.

k. Miscellaneous Measuring Gages
  (1) Purpose
    (a) Thickness (Feeler) Gages
      These gages are fixed in leaf form, which permits the checking and measuring of small openings such as contact points, narrow slots, and so forth. They are widely used to check the flatness of parts in straightening and grinding operations and in squaring objects with a try square.
    (b) Wire and Drill Gages
      The wire gage is used for gaging metal wire, and a similar gage is also used to check the size of hot and cold rolled steel, sheet and plate iron, and music wire. Drill gages determine the size of a drill and indicate the correct size of drill to use for given tap size. Drill number and decimal size are also shown in this type gage.
    (c) Drill Rods or Blanks
      Drill rods or blanks are used on line inspection work to check the size of drilled holes in the same manner as with plug gages. They are also used for setup inspection to check the location of holes.
    (d) Thread Gages
      Among the many gages used in connection with the machining and inspection of threads are the center gage and the screw pitch gages.
      1. Center gage
        The center gage is used to set thread cutting tools. Four scales on the gage are used for determining the number of threads per inch.
      2. Screw pitch gage
        Screw pitch gages are used to determine the pitch of an unknown thread. The pitch of a screw thread is the distance between the center of one tooth to the center of the next tooth.
    (e) Small Hole Gage Set
      This set of 4 or more gages is used to check dimensions of small holes, slots, groves etc., from approximately 1/8 to 1/2" in diameter.

8

  (f) Telescoping Gages
   These gages are used for measuring the inside size of slots or holes up to 6" in width or diameter.
  (g) Thread Cutting Tool Gages
   These gages provide a standard for thread cutting tools. They have an enclosed angle of 29 and include a 29 setting tool. One gage furnishes the correct form for square threads and the other for Acme standard threads.
  (h) Fillet and Radius Gages
   These gages are used to check convex and concave radii in corners or against shoulders.
  (i) Drill Point Gage
   This gage is used to check the accuracy of drill cutting edges after grinding. It is also equipped with a 6" hook rule. This tool can be used as a drill point gage, hook rule, plain rule, and a slide caliper for taking outside measurements.
  (j) Marking Gages
   A marking gage is used to mark off guidelines parallel to an edge, end, or surface of a piece of wood. It has a sharp spur or pin that does the marking.
  (k) Tension Gage
   This type of gage is used to check contact point pressure and brush spring tension in 1 ounce graduations.
  (l) Saw Tooth Micrometer Gage
   This special gage checks the depth of saw teeth in thousandths of an inch from 0 to 0.075 inch.

III. NONEDGED TOOLS
  1. General

    This title encompasses a large group of general purpose hand-tools. These tools are termed nonedged hand-tools because they are not used for cutting purposes and do not have sharpened or cutting edges. They are designed to facilitate mechanical operations such as clamping, hammering, twisting, turning, etc. This group includes such tools as hammers, mallets, and screwdrivers; which are commonly referred to as driving tools. Other types of nonedged tools are wrenches, pliers, clamps, pullers, soldering irons, torches, and many others of similar nature. Several types of pliers have cutting edges (exceptions to the rule).

  2. Useful Nonedged Tools
   a. Hammers and Mallets
    (1) Purpose
     Hammers and mallets are used to drive nails, spikes, drift pins, bolts, and wedges. They are also used to strike chisels, punches, and to shape metals. Sledge hammers are used to drive spikes and large nails, to break rock and concrete, and to drift heavy timbers.
   b. Screwdrivers
    (1) Purpose

Screwdrivers are used for driving or removing screws or bolts with slotted or special heads.

c. Wrenches
   (1) Purpose
   Wrenches are used to tighten or loosen nuts, bolts, screws, and pipe plugs. Special wrenches are made to grip round stock, such as pipe, studs, and rods. Spanner wrenches are used to turn cover plates, rings and couplings.

d. Pliers and Tongs
   (1) Purpose
   Pliers are used for gripping, cutting, bending, forming, or holding work, and for special jobs. Tongs look like long-handled pliers and are mainly used for holding or handling hot pieces of metal work to be forged or quenched, or hot pieces of glass.

e. Clamping Devices
   (1) Purpose
   Vises are used for holding work on the bench when it is being planed, sawed, drilled, shaped, sharpened, riveted, or when wood is being glued. Clamps are used for holding work that cannot be satisfactorily held in a vise because of its shape or size, or when a vise is not available. Clamps are generally used for light work.

f. Jacks
   (1) Purpose
   Jacks are used to raise or lower work and heavy loads short distances. Some jacks are used for pushing and pulling operations, or for spreading and clamping.

g. Bars and Mattock
   (1) Purpose
   Bars are heavy steel tools used to lift and move heavy objects and to pry where leverage is needed. They are also used to remove nails and spikes during wrecking operations. The mattock is used for digging in hard ground, cutting Toots irnderground, und to loosen clay formations in which there is little or no rock. The mattock may also be used for light prying when no bars are available,

h. Soldering Irons
   (1) Purpose
   Soldering is joining two pieces of metal by adhesion. The soldering iron is the source of heat by melting solder and heating the parts to be joined to the proper temperature.

i. Grinders and Sharpening Stones
   (1) Purpose
   Grinders are devices that are designed to mount abrasive wheels that will wear away other materials to varying degrees. Special grinders are designed to receive engine valves. Sharpening stones are used for whetting or final sharpening of sharp edged tools that have been ground to shape or to a fine point on a grinder,

j. Benders and Pullers
   (1) Purpose

Benders are designed to facilitate bending brass or copper pipe and tubing. Pullers are designed to facilitate pulling operations such as removing bearings, gears, wheels, pulleys, sheaves, bushings, cylinder sleeves, shafts, and other close-fitting parts.

- k. Torches
  - (1) Purpose
    Torches are used as sources of heat in soldering, sweating, tinning, burning, and other miscellaneous jobs where heat is required.
- l. Blacksmith's Anvils and Iron Working Tools
  - (1) Purpose
    Blacksmith's anvils are designed to provide a working surface when punching holes through metal and for supporting the metal when it is being forged and shaped. Iron working tools such as flatters, fullers, swages, hardies, and set hammers are used to form or shape forgings. Heading tools are used to shape bolts.
- m. Breast Drill and Ratchet Bit Brace
  - (1) Purpose
    The breast drill and ratchet bit brace are used to hold various kinds of bits and twist drills used in boring and reaming holes and to drive screws, nuts, and bolts.
- n. Sheet Metal Tools
  - (1) Purpose
    Sheet metal working tools consist of stakes, dolly blocks, calking tools, rivet sets, and dolly bars. Punches, shears, and hammers are also sheet metal working tools. However, they are covered in other sections of this text. Rivet sets and dolly bars are used to form heads on rivets after joining sections of sheet metal and steel work. Stakes are used to support sheet metal while the metal is being shaped. Calking tools are used to shape joints of sheet metal. Dolly blocks are used conjunction with bumping body hammers to straighten out damaged sheet metal.

IV. EDGED HANDTOOLS
  1. General
    Edged handtools are designed with sharp edges for working on metal, wood, plastic, leather, cloth, glass, and other materials. They are used to remove portions from the work or to separate the work into sections by cutting, punching, scraping, chiseling, filing, and so forth.
  2. Useful Edged Eandtools
    a. Chisels
      (1) Purpose
        Chisels are made to cut wood, metal hard putty, and other materials. Woodworker's chisels are used to pare off and cut wood. Cold chisels are used to chip and cut cold metal. Some blacksmith's chisels are used to cut hot metal. A special chisel that is available is used to cut hard putty so that glass may be removed from its frame channel.
    b. Files
      (1) Purpose

Files are used for cutting, smoothing off, or removing small amounts of metal.

c. Knives

   (1) Purpose

   Most knives are used to cut, pare, notch, and trim wood, leather, rubber, and other materials. Some knives used by glaziers are called putty knives; these are used to apply and spread putty when installing glass.

d. Scrapers

   (1) Purpose

   Some scrapers are used for trueing metal, wood, and plastic surfaces which have previously been machined or filed. Other scrapers are made to remove paint, stencil markings, and other coatings from various surfaces.

e. Punches

   (1) Purpose

   Punches are used to punch holes in metal, leather, paper, and other materials; mark metal, drive pins or rivets; to free frozen pins from their holes; and aline holes in different sections of metal. Special punches are designed to install grommets and snap fasteners. Bench mounted punching machines are used to punch holes in metal one at a time, or up to 12 holes simultaneously.

f. Awls

   (1) Purpose

   A saddler's awl is used for forcing holes in cloth or leather to make sewing easier. A scratch awl is used for making a center point or a small hole and for scribing lines on wood and plastics.

g. Shears, Nippers, and Pincers

   (1) Purpose

   Shears are used for cutting sheet metal and steel of various thicknesses and shapes. Nippers are used to cut metal off flush with a surface, and likewise to cut wire, light metal bars, bolts, and nails. Pincers are used to pull out nails, bolts, and pins.

h. Bolt, Cable, and Glass Cutters

   (1) Purpose

   Cutters or clippers are used to cut bolts, rods, wire rope, cable, screws, rivets, nuts, bars, strips, and wire. Special cutters are made to cut glass.

i. Piper and Tube Cutters, and Flaring Tools

   (1) Purpose

   Pipe cutters are used to cut pipe made of steel, brass, copper, wrought iron, and lead. Tube cutters are used to cut tube made of iron, steel, brass, copper, and aluminum. The essential difference is that tubing has considerably thinner walls are compared to pipe. Flaring tools are used to make single or double flares in the ends of tubing,

j. Reamers

   (1) Purpose

Reamers are used to smoothly enlarge drilled holes to an exact size and to finish the hole at the same time. Reamers are also used to remove burrs from the inside diameters of pipe and drilled holes,

k. Taps and Dies
   (1)   Purpose

Taps and dies are used to cut threads in metal, plastics, or hard rubber. The taps are used for cutting internal threads, and the dies are used to cut external threads.

l. Thread Chasers
   (1)   Purpose

Thread chasers are used to re-thread damaged external or internal threads,

m. Screw and Tap Extractors
   (1)   Purpose

Screw extractors are used to remove broken screws without damaging the surrounding material or the threaded hole. Tap extractors are used to remove broken taps.

www.ingramcontent.com/pod-product-compliance
Lightning Source LLC
Chambersburg PA
CBHW082045300426
44117CB00015B/2623